MR. CLUTCH: The Jerry West Story

MR. CLUTCH
The Jerry West Story

Jerry West with Bill Libby

An Associated Features Book

Published by Prentice-Hall, Inc., Englewood Cliffs, New Jersey

Fifth printing. . . . . October, 1971

Mr. Clutch: The Jerry West Story
by Jerry West with Bill Libby

Library of Congress Catalog Card Number: 73-82904

13-604710-6

Printed in the United States of America • T

Prentice-Hall International, Inc., London
Prentice-Hall of Australia, Pty. Ltd., Sydney
Prentice-Hall of Canada, Ltd., Toronto
Prentice-Hall of India Private Ltd., New Delhi
Prentice-Hall of Japan, Inc., Tokyo

For my family, which has put up with me
even though I did not always make it easy.

ACKNOWLEDGMENTS

For their help in the preparation of this book, I wish to thank my mother and wife; Dick Polen and Hank LaBrie; A. L. "Shorty" Hardman of the Charleston Gazette; Dick Hudson of the Charleston Daily Mail; Jack Kent Cooke, Fred Schaus, Chick Hearn, Rod Hundley and Jim Brochu of the Los Angeles Lakers; Bill van Breda Kolff; Wen Roberts of Photography, Inc.; Merv Harris, and editors Zander Hollander and Dave Schulz of Associated Features Inc.

Jerry West

Contents

Contents

MR. CLUTCH: The Jerry West Story

Prologue

It is a very special agony Jerry West endures around one hundred times a year.

He is a tall, thin person, boyishly handsome. He has brownish-blond hair, pale skin, clear blue eyes, and a nose which has been broken into an irregular line. He speaks softly and seldom, with a slightly southern nasal twang. He is conservative and shy and very polite. He is absolutely dedicated to his profession.

He is a basketball player. He has been playing the game competitively since he was twelve years old and now he is past thirty. He began playing it in junior high school and high school in a small town in West Virginia and continued at the state university. He played it in the Pan-American Games in Chicago and the Olympic Games in Rome. Now he plays it as a professional in Los Angeles.

For eight months a season, from September through April, he plays on the average of every other night and sometimes three or four nights in a row in Los Angeles, Seattle, San Diego, San Francisco, Phoenix, Chicago, Milwaukee, Detroit, Cincinnati, Atlanta, Baltimore, Philadelphia, New York, Boston, and wherever a game is scheduled.

He is always coming from somewhere and going someplace else, moving in and out of the sunshine of southern California and the deep South and the snowy cold of the Midwest and East, living out of a suitcase, eating on the run, grabbing sleep wherever he can, killing time in airports and hotels, riding cabs through the busy cities to the great arenas.

1

The agony starts when he wakes up in the morning and begins to wait for the game nine or ten hours away. He thinks about the game and waits for the game. The tension thickens through the long day. The hours pass slowly.

At home, he grows restless and edgy and begins to snap at his wife and shout at his three sons, and gets out of the house every chance he can. On the road, he wears away his impatience kidding with his teammates, playing cards, watching television, walking the lonely streets of strange towns.

He tries to nap, but usually can't, stirring nervously in his bed, taking a pill to ease the tension. He tries to eat, but often can't, sick to his stomach from the suspense. As early as is reasonable, he flees to the arena.

Things are better there, in the dressing room with the smell of liniment and the chatter and the busy business of taping injuries and getting dressed with the other players, who know what this thing is for him. It is not good, but it is better.

He pulls on the gold and purple uniform number 44 of the Los Angeles Lakers, ties up his basketball shoes and sits on a stool and waits away those last awful moments. Frequently he swallows pills to calm his stomach because by now he is so nervous he feels he may vomit.

He has been playing this game for a long time and he is used to it and very good at it, one of the greatest of all time, but it is only a little different for him now than it was for him in the beginning. He is a nervous person, a perfectionist worked up with the desire to win every game.

Finally, the coach speaks to the team, telling them what he wants them to do, slowly and calmly at first, then faster and more excitedly, building up his emotion, striving to stimulate them.

The coach's hands clap loudly in the quiet room and the players shout and run out through the passageway and onto the court. It is better here, with the ball in his hands, practicing, while the large crowd files enthusiastically into the great arena.

It is best when the ball is thrown up and the game finally begins with an explosion of running feet and reaching arms and angled elbows and springy leaps and colliding bodies and arched shots. He can lose himself in this swift action, concentrating on the nine other players and the two officials, the colors of their uniforms blurring as they scramble around the narrow confines of the court, which cuts them off from the crowd, hearing the squeal of sneakered feet on the hardwood, the thump of the basketball bouncing on the floor or off the glass backboards, the sharp, piercing whistles of the referees, the muttered profanities of the players, the pleading shouts of the coaches, who strain at the boundaries of their benches, the clack of the typewriters along press row, the noise of the fans washing over them.

There may have been or may be better players, though there can not have been many. There may be bigger, stronger, faster, possibly even more skilled players, but it is doubtful anyone ever has played this game harder. West starts, stops, runs again, dribbles, passes, takes a pass, cuts, jumps, shoots, blocks a shot, hounds his man, steals the ball at both ends of the court with every ounce of energy in his skinny body for every second of the 40 or more minutes he plays out of the 48 minutes in every pro game.

He goes up for a shot, is fouled and knocked down hard, pushes himself erect, pushes aside the passing pain, walks to the free throw line, draws a deep breath, and pushes two shots home. He runs back to defense at the other end, moves in for a rebound, is hipped off stride and out of the play. He recovers to take a lead pass in full stride, pounds full-out downcourt and lays one up and in. He hurries back on defense, chases his man, lunges for the ball, steals it, begins to move with it, kicks it out of bounds, punches his fist and shakes his head in disgust, moves back again. Trying to cut off a drive, he collides with a foe and draws a foul. He glares at the ref, bites his lip, holds his tongue and his temper. A moment later, the ball is passed to him on offense, he jumps and arches in a shot.

He stands out shooting, making a quick, dribbling move to his right, stopping suddenly, jumping swiftly, cocking the ball back on the palm of one hand, then gently arching a soft shot toward the basket, which swishes through the cords.

Bill Sharman has said, "He's the greatest player at both ends of the court the game has ever seen." Bob Pettit has said, "He's the greatest clutch shooter ever." Bill Russell has said, "You can't stop him. Forget it." Len Wilkens has said, "If there's a way to beat you, West will find it." After the 1969 NBA play-offs, a football coach, Tommy Prothro, said, "He's the greatest athlete alive." One of Jerry's greatest rivals, John Havlicek, said, "He is the master. You can talk about others, but he is the one. He is the only guard." And John's teammate Tom Sanders asked, "Do you spell that g-o-d?"

He is an exceptionally graceful player and in his most magnificent moments he is like a ballet dancer among brutes. It is not an easy game, especially the pro game, played by giants, played very rough. At 6-3, he is smaller than most, less rugged. As he plays, he begins to sweat and tire. He seems expressionless, but there is a drawn severity to the muscles of his face; his mouth gapes open as he gasps for breath and there is a light burning bright in his eyes, an intense, passionate light that reflects an awesome dedication.

In his first eight seasons as a pro, he has had his nose broken half a dozen times, his thumb broken, his hand broken twice, teeth knocked out, his eyeball bruised, his hip bruised, joints and muscles twisted and sprained, pulled and torn. He has been beaten black and blue many times, slashed and cut, had the wind knocked out of him, been knocked unconscious. He has missed 10, 20, 30 games some seasons. But he also has played almost every game some seasons.

When he cannot play, he suffers on the sidelines, watching others in his place, unable to help his team win, which he is paid well to do. He curses his injuries and tosses through sleepless nights, despairing and considering retirement, which he hates to think about, when he is called fragile or injury-prone and when people say he can't be counted on. Often he limps back into action long before he should, and is frustrated then by not being able to play as well as he can.

He can't even stand to be rested on the bench in brief breaks during games in which he is playing. He leans forward, watching the action intently, shouting at his teammates, wrestling with his hands, impatient to be out on the court again. Then he is back in, moving and lunging and crashing around again.

The older the game gets, the younger he seems to get. As the climax draws near, he stifles his exhaustion and seems to gather himself for a great effort. He is that rarest of men, who improve under pressure. He is at his best when it counts the most. Nothing finer can be said about any athlete than that he is a great clutch performer and Jerry West probably is the best basketball has ever had, possibly the best any sport has ever had. The chances are he has won more games in the last moments than any athlete ever.

He is furious with his failures, but he has done much in a fruitless attempt to avert them. He has scored better every season in the playoffs than he did in the regular season. He has the highest scoring average of any player in the history of the playoffs.

If his team has won, it is fine for him, finally, when the game has ended and he has pushed through the crowd and worked his way into the dressing room. If his team has lost, it is no good and he begins right away to wait for the next game, when they may win. Or if he has played poorly, which he does sometimes, it is bad and he thinks about his next time, when he may play better.

He sinks onto a stool, glassy-eyed, red-eyed from the smoke in the arena, his uniform stained with sweat, his chest heaving from lack of breath, his muscles still quivering under his damp skin. He sits in the dressing room, noisy in victory, quiet in defeat, and you sense the relief in him, the ebbing of his passion, the lessening of that glint in his eye, the softening of his drawn expression.

The reporters come in and he speaks politely to them, but he is not good with them. He does not express himself easily and he is afraid of saying the wrong thing. If his team has won, he very carefully says what are supposed to be the right things, playing down his role, praising his teammates, praising his opponents. If his team has lost, or if he has played poorly, he says little, excuses himself and shuts up, considering and brooding over what might have been done differently. Few ever have been more dedicated to perfection. He is almost always dissatisfied—especially, of course, in defeat.

Slowly he gathers himself, strips off his sweaty, soiled uniform and goes to shower, to steam away some of the aches. He emerges, towels his flushed skin, brushes his hair, pulls on a neat but conservative suit, and goes out of the room then, into the night. If the team is on the road, he rides with the others to the hotel or the airport. If the team is at home he goes to where those close to the team wait for the players, kisses his wife, walks with her to the car, and they drive home.

It is not so bad then, the excitement dissipated, the sickness passed. He talks to his wife. At home he looks in on his children. Perhaps he has a sandwich and a glass of milk or a soft drink. He is gentle then, thoughtful, considerate. If it has not gone well, he will be more quiet than usual. Either way, it will be a while before he unwinds completely. He may have to take a sleeping pill in order to sleep through the night. He hates taking pills. He thinks it's stupid and dangerous. But he does it because he doesn't know any other way to survive.

He will be all right then until the day of his next game, which may be the next night, when the very special agony will begin all over again.

Jerry West was born and raised a poor country boy in a small town in West Virginia, a small, awkward, lonely boy, who lacked confidence, but was driven by ambition. He grew up tall and straight and agile to become a high school all-star, a college All-American, an Olympic gold-medal winner, and an All-Pro, a rich young man who is singled out as a celebrity from Broadway to the Sunset Strip.

He is considered one of the greatest players ever to play his game. He makes 100,000 dollars a year. He has a beautiful wife and three handsome, healthy sons. He has a fine home and drives a fancy car. He probably is secure for life. Yet he is not greatly different from what he was 20 years ago.

He is still something of a loner, shy and nervous. He has done much more and has much more than most, yet he sets such high goals for himself that he is discontented with himself, and he seems always afraid he will lose what he has.

He is so straight he is considered an All-American boy, which distresses him because he feels that he is not that good. Yet he is the sort of person men say they want their sons to be. "He sets high standards and goes after them fiercely," the late Laker manager Lou Mohs once said. "If I wanted a son to be a certain way, I'd pattern him after Jerry and I wouldn't change a thing." Mohs added, "Under intense pressure, most people's bodies go out of kilter. Under intense pressure, Jerry's reactions sharpen. He is that rarest of human beings who can do more when it counts the most." Frank McGuire said, "He has the greatest heart of any player I've seen." Joe Lapchick said, "West is everything a coach could want."

He is one of the great athletes of all time. And he is a fine, if imperfect, person. He is also a complex and sensitive person. It is not easy for him to speak of others, none of whom he wishes to offend. It is not easy for him to look at himself objectively and point out heroic deeds and compliment himself. It is not easy for him to include the details of personal statistics and scores and honors which illuminate the games and seasons of his career, but which embarrass him. This book did not come easy to Jerry. But, then, nothing ever has.

Bill Libby

1
Zeke from Cabin Creek

I think I became a basketball player because it is a game a boy can play by himself. I've always been the sort of person who likes to be by himself some. I've always been a guy who lives inside of himself a lot. I can't stand to give too much of myself away to others. It's not that I don't care for others. I have cared and do care for many. It's just that I've always been shy and I've never had a lot of confidence.

That may sound strange since I've become something sort of special in sports, but it's true. I'm my own worst critic. I'm not very easily satisfied, and I'm not always at ease with other people. Eventually, basketball becomes a game you play with a team against other teams. And I stayed with it because I loved it and became good at it. But I think in the beginning I turned to it because I could practice it alone.

A neighbor put up a hoop in his backyard and my best memory of my boyhood is me out there all alone dribbling and shooting in all kinds of weather, even when it was raining or snowing or real cold, until it got too dark to see, until my Mom would whip me for coming home late and missing supper.

I was born Jerry Alan West on May 28, 1938, in the town of Cheylan in Kanawha County, West Virginia, about 14 miles south of Charleston. Around five hundred persons lived in Cheylan. I went to high school in East Bank, about four miles away. Our post office was in Cabin Creek, which was our mailing address, and from this I got my nickname, "Zeke from Cabin Creek." I don't remember who gave it to me. Maybe the Laker broadcaster, Chick Hearn. Maybe one of the Laker players. I'm stuck with it, I guess, but I never liked it. To me, it makes me sound like a hillbilly. And I'm sure it's meant that way, even if not in a mean way, though I don't think I think of it the way outsiders do. In West Virginia, we're "mountaineers," but few of us are barefoot and dirty.

Much of West Virginia has such natural beauty it's been called "the Switzerland of the U.S." Parts of Kanawha County and other nearby areas are hilly and rugged, but really beautiful.

Cheylan is a country town, but nice. There are many pleasant houses. There are woods, where I used to hunt, and a stream, where I used to fish. The water was dirty, and I wasn't a good swimmer. I didn't swim there.

The people there lived a nice, quiet life. There were some factories and some coal mines, some of which have closed down, unfortunately. In recent years, there has been a lot of depression in West Virginia. Times have been hard and there has been a lot of poverty. I'd be lying if I said otherwise. There are people living such a hard life in parts of West Virginia that it just breaks your heart to see them. But this gives others a distorted view of the state and those who live there.

Most of the people in West Virginia are working and leading decent lives, just like the people in New York or Illinois or California. Most of the people in Cheylan have found work at a DuPont plant or a power company or a glass company or other places in the area, or in Charleston, and their lives are not really all that different from the lives of people elsewhere.

It's been written that my father, Howard West, was a coal miner, but this is not true. He worked almost 27 years as a machine operator at the Pure Oil place until the crude oil wells ran dry and it shut down. He decided he wanted to go into business for himself and bought a gas station in Mineral Wells, near Parkersburg, and when I was 10 we moved there, but we didn't stay long. Mom says we stayed just long enough for our money to run out. Anyway, while we were there I was very homesick, but when Dad gave up the gas station we moved back to Cheylan. He got a job as an electrician in a coal company shop. Eventually he retired.

He died of a heart attack in 1963. He worked very hard all his life and he never made much more than $5,000 a year. Six thousand was a real good year. We didn't have much, but we always had clean clothes and there always was food on the table.

Our first home in Cheylan had six rooms. When we moved back, we got a place with nine rooms. These were plain, two-story wooden houses, but they were fine. Kids don't think about those things much. This was where we lived and that was it.

The second place burned down in 1963, right after my father died, which made things even more difficult for Mom. All our possessions, including my scrapbooks and trophies and even the gold medal I won for playing basketball for the United States in the Olympics in Rome in 1960, were destroyed.

Mom has another place there now, where she still lives, with my sister Barbara, who is 21 and is a scholarship student at the University, majoring in chemistry.

There were six children in our family. First-born was a girl, Patricia, who is now Mrs. Jack Noel; she works as a postmistress and has two children. Then came a boy, Charles, who is treasurer of a company in Charleston, is married, and has two children. Then came David, who was killed in Korea when I was a teen-ager. He was a Master Sergeant, a forward observer for a mortar group. He was a year past the time for his rotation back to the States. His death hit all of us real hard. He was the older brother I tagged after a lot and I

really missed him when he went into the Army and then
when he died. After David came Hannah, who is now Mrs.
Calvin Lilly and has three children. Then I came, and then
Barbara.

I really can't say we were a real close family. Dad worked
hard and he was tired when he came home. He wasn't much
interested in sports and he was very strict. And I didn't con-
fide in Mom or Dad much. The closest brother to me, David,
was seven or eight years older than I was, and he was gone
before I even got into high school. I had some good friends,
but I wasn't real close to anyone. I had an older friend who
used to take me hunting sometimes. And my brother-in-law
took me to ball games at the University or in Cincinnati
sometimes. Mostly, I did things by myself.

I wanted things I didn't have. I'd work, doing odd jobs,
like cutting lawns for a dollar or a dollar-and-a-half, to get
things I wanted, like some clothes, or a fishing pole, or money
for the movies. I was very aware that we didn't have some
of the things some of the others had. We had no car, for example. Without a car, I wasn't too anxious to take girls out.
I only had two or three dates all the time I was in high
school, even after I became a star, when it would have been
easy. I was bashful. I didn't have much and I felt bad about
it. I was small and skinny in my early teens. I was very
self-conscious and shy, almost backward. I'm not the most
secure person in the world, even today.

I remember being by myself a lot. I'd get an old boat and
go fishing for bass and catfish. Later on I'd go a long way up
in the mountains to fish for trout. I'd borrow a gun and go
to the woods to shoot squirrels or rabbits. In time I raised
the money to buy my own gun. I still like hunting and fishing,
even when I'm by myself. It's something a man can do
alone and quiet, out with nature. It's something I was raised
with and am used to.

I always loved sports. I saved baseball cards. Stan Musial
and Ted Williams were two of my heroes, though the Cincinnati Reds were the team we got on the radio and the team

most of the people in West Virginia followed. Pro football and pro basketball weren't very big in those days, at least not around West Virginia. I followed the high school teams and the University teams. I remember listening to the University basketball games on the radio.

And I remember very vividly going to see the University play a basketball game against Clemson. Mark Workman, one of the University's first All-Americans, was on the team then. We sat way high and the court seemed very far away and the players seemed very small, but I was really thrilled. In fact, it was one of the highlights of my life. I can remember imagining myself playing down there on the court some day, though I was so small I don't think I really believed it could happen. I wanted very much to think some day I could get to be someone and have something.

I went home and imitated all the different players, imagining I was them, practicing in that neighbor's court all by myself. When I started on that court I was so small and the ball seemed so heavy, I had to shoot two-handed and underhanded, throwing the ball up from between my legs with all of my might just to get it up to the basket. As I grew it got easier, but I grew slowly. When I was 11 or 12 I was only about 5-6 and didn't even weigh 100 pounds. I was so small, the other kids wouldn't let me play football with them, and I'd wind up back on my basketball court.

Actually, football was my first love, but when I got to junior high school and tried out for the football team, I was so small they didn't have a uniform little enough to fit me. I wasn't good enough, anyway, and wound up as the team manager. I played some sandlot baseball—we didn't have any Little League or anything like that—but I wasn't very good at that, either. I tried out for track once in high school, but didn't make that, either. As it turned out, the only sport I wound up playing in high school was basketball, but for quite a while that looked pretty doubtful, too.

Duke Shaver was the basketball coach at Cheylan Junior High School. He was a fine man, very inspirational to the

young people, and a good coach, very strong on condition-
ing. He used to make us duck-walk and do other tough exercises. He used to run us a lot and stress our getting back on
defense. Like most kids, I liked to goof off, but I think the
stress he put on an athlete staying in shape stuck with me
and was one of the real contributing factors to my eventual
success.

Success came slow though, or so it seemed at the time. In
the seventh grade, I only got to dress for one or two games
and didn't play at all. I was very nervous and didn't see any
hope at all for me as a basketball player, but I kept trying.
By the eighth grade, I had grown a little and I got to play
a little, but not very much. I was always crushed when I
didn't get to play. I wanted to, real badly.

By the ninth grade, I not only got to play as a regular
starter, but I was elected captain, which was a thrill. Then all
those long hours practicing alone began to pay off.

I didn't know much about playing basketball, but I could
shoot some and I averaged 13 points a game. I shot two-
handed set-shots from way out then. I don't even think I could
shoot two-handed now. Anyway, I began to think maybe
I'd make a basketball player after all. No one at home en-
couraged me. I was on my own. I was very dedicated, though
I really wasn't thinking much beyond playing high school ball.

In the summer of 1953, between my ninth and 10th grades
in school, just before I began at East Bank High, I shot up
six inches. It was unbelievable. It was like I was walking on
stilts. I was so clumsy, I couldn't control myself. I used to
fall down stairs all the time. I used to fall down just walking
through the house. My mother was afraid I'd hurt myself.
She couldn't keep me in clothes. She'd scrape up the money
for a new pair of pants for me and two weeks later they'd
be too small.

It was fine for basketball; suddenly I was a six-footer. But
it was hard on me, personally. I was skinny as a rail and so
self-conscious it was painful. I can't imagine growing up to be
6-8 or 6-10 or a seven-footer. I mean it's fine to be a Wilt

Chamberlain or a Bill Russell, but it must be very hard to adjust psychologically to being that much taller than everyone else, and if you don't have their kind of ability at sports, it must be a very hard burden to bear.

The basketball coach at East Bank was Roy Williams, who died in 1968. He was an exceptional coach, in some ways the best I ever had. He stressed fundamentals, defense, and team play. This was what I needed. Under his guidance I first began to become a well-rounded player.

I don't care how well you can shoot, if you can't play the rest of the game you're not really going to go very far, certainly not to the pro game. Again, the lessons I learned have stayed with me all my life.

Building a basketball player is like building anything else— you start with the foundation. If the foundation is solid, the rest will be more solid. I don't say a natural athlete can't pick up what he needs later, but I think it gets harder as you go along.

I think I became an exceptional basketball player because I began practicing when I was so young and so small I could hardly lift the ball and because I got good coaching in school and got that good foundation and never stopped playing and working at the game. I am not as good a player as I might have been had I worked harder and got an even better foundation, but I am very fortunate that things were as they were for me.

In my first year at East Bank, my sophomore season, I got to play very little. We had a fair team and there was not really much room for a new player to break in, and I just wasn't all that outstanding then. I played in only eight games and didn't even get to dress some of the time, which really hurt me and didn't do my confidence any good.

I've looked it all up to jog my memory and I'll give some of the details and the statistics, which I guess are important.

I played for the first time in my team's fourth game, against Charleston High at home on January 1, 1954. I didn't score. The only big night I had that season came when three regulars were out with bad colds and they had to use me. I scored 12 points as we beat visiting DuPont. My sophomore season ended in our twelfth game, against visiting Beckley. I broke my ankle.

I had scored a couple of baskets and was playing well, I remember, when I went up to try to block a shot and came down on the side of my foot. I felt something snap and it hurt real bad. I went out, but the coach thought it was only a sprained ankle and tried to tape it so I could continue playing. But I could hardly walk on it, much less run on it, so that was it for that game and, as it turned out, for that season. It hurt so bad I couldn't sleep that night. In the morning I walked a mile on it to the doctor's office. He examined me and told me I had broken some bones in my ankle and would have to wear a cast for a while and wouldn't be able to play any more basketball that season. I was broken-hearted. And I was a little scared it might affect my future play, too. But I didn't let on about that.

The Pioneers, as we were called, managed just fine without me, winding up with a 16-4 record and winning two games in the West Virginia State tournament sectionals before losing in the second and final regional game.

The doctor had put what they call a walking cast on my foot, so I could continue going to school, hobbling about. Like most kids, I was kind of proud of the cast and it made me sort of a hero in a funny way. My friends signed the cast and drew pictures on it. I clowned around in it and kept breaking it. The doctor couldn't understand it and kept asking me if I was sure I wasn't doing what I wasn't supposed to be doing, and I kept assuring him of course I wasn't.

I remember once I was fooling around in the gym and I went tumbling off balance back through the double doors and flat on my back in the hallway. When I looked up, who was looking down on me but the principal! He didn't care much for my idea of fun. It was the only fun that was left to me. Far from having attained stardom, I finished my first season of varsity basketball as the sad-sack manager of my team.

2
King of the Hill

Once the cast came off my leg and the ankle felt all right, I really got serious about basketball. That summer, after school ended, I played day or night, rain or snow, with anyone I could find to play, and by myself if I couldn't find anyone.

Every one of the previous season's regulars had been a senior and had graduated, so we didn't figure to have a very good team, but I knew I would get to play, possibly even as a starter, and I was very anxious to make the most of the opportunity. When school started in September, I couldn't wait for football season to end and basketball season to begin. I wasn't a bad student, but all I really cared about was basketball. I wasn't even terribly interested in girls. I was still skinny and gawky and awfully introverted, but I loved playing basketball and I didn't feel inhibited on the court.

I've always been able to lose myself in the games, to concentrate on the play, which I think is very important. If you're worried about the crowd, if you hear what the fans yell, if you're thinking about how you look or what you're going to do after the game, it's bound to take a lot away from your performance. I think you can develop some concentration by applying yourself to it, but it came natural to me and helped me a lot.

When the season did come, finally, it was more than I hoped for, personally, but less than I hoped for as a member of the team.

It was my senior year in high school; the first time I experienced some real pressure. CHARLESTON DAILY MAIL

I won a regular berth at forward, but we won only eleven of twenty-three games, one of only three times in 15 years my teams had a losing record. Personally, I averaged 24 points a game and had 37 in one and 38 in another. In one I hit 15 out of 19 shots from the field although my foes were hanging all over me all through the game.

I had switched from two-handed sets and was working exclusively on one-handed jumpers and it was coming fast. I'd always practiced the one-handers, which is all anyone uses these days anyway, and as I matured they began to work very well. I was green and I didn't know anything about getting loose for shots or getting around a defensive man on drives, but I was learning, and it didn't really matter that much because my opponents were green and didn't know much about defensing a shooter and didn't give me that much trouble.

I know this may be hard to believe, but I honestly think that I was a better pure shooter in high school than I was to become at any point later in my career. I can't exactly explain it, except maybe that I was young and flexible and had very good rhythm and wasn't always worried about the other aspects of my game. I had a good eye and a light touch and I could pop the ball up on the rim real soft, where it would roll through if it didn't swish.

I was by no means a good all-around basketball player. There is a lot more to basketball than just shooting, and the rest of it is a lot harder than shooting. I had good spring and timing and I wasn't afraid, so I was a pretty good rebounder. I didn't run into a lot of players who were much taller than me, though a lot of them were huskier. But I didn't handle the ball real well, and my dribbling and passing and my instinct for making the right moves just hadn't been developed yet.

After all, I was just a kid, and the fact is, honestly, that I am still learning, every game, every season. Maybe these things come natural to an Oscar Robertson, but most of us have to

take what we have and work at them all the time. I wasn't
even a good free throw shooter, which I did become. I had
games where I missed six or seven free throws in a row,
which is inexcusable. But I just hadn't grooved my form yet.
And I wasn't a good all-around shooter. But I could pop
those one-handed jumpers like mad.

We played in what was I think the toughest area for high
school basketball in the state, and as a team we were just
plain outclassed most of the way. We had a couple of big wins
and scored a couple of big upsets, but we took some bad
beatings that season and had trouble winning as many games
as we lost. Beckley beat us by 26 points, South Charleston
by 29 points, and Huntington by 33 points. Even if you personally have scored your share, it's depressing to walk into
the locker room after losses like that, and it's hard to hold
your head up in the school corridor the next day.

I've never been one to take defeat lightly. I know it's a
cliché to say you hate to lose and I know all athletes say it,
but I've also known many athletes on every level, from
high school through pro, who couldn't care less, and some
who don't even care what they themselves do. It's a sort of
mean thing to say, but I want to say what I really feel,
which I have not always done in interviews. You say the
right thing and say the right thing, and the time just comes
where you know you should say what you really feel, and
this is it.

I hate guys who don't hate to lose, who put themselves
ahead of the team, or who put themselves ahead of the game.
I just don't know how to be that way. I'd really hate like
heck to score only one or two baskets in a game, but if we
won I'd feel a lot better than if I scored 10 or 20 baskets
and we lost, and that's the truth. Basketball is one of the
team games and you have to put yourself behind the team.

I'm a shooter and it's always been my job to shoot, but
when it wasn't the right time, I just didn't do it. And if I
needed two points to wind up with 20,000 points on the last

night of my career, and a shot at that point might cost my team the game, I just wouldn't take the shot, and I mean that. I might feel bad the rest of my life that I didn't get the 20,000, but I'd feel good that I had known it wasn't right to go for it.

It's always a little easier to accept defeat when you know you're being beaten by better teams, which we were that year, but it was still tough to take. We did surprise a lot of people by winning the sectional, although I'm not proud of my performance in my first tournament.

We won our first two games and the sectional easily, although I fouled out early and wound up with only 11 points in the opener. Then in the first game of the regionals we played a team, Nitro, we had beaten by 20 points during the season, and we had them beat easily by 15 points at halftime this time, but we were sent into a stall early and lost our momentum and they came on to beat us, 50-47. I had a good first half, but scored only four points in that heart-breaking second half. I think if what you're doing is working, you should keep on doing it until it stops working. I learned that night that it is disastrous to disrupt your rhythm.

My performance in that final game, and my team's performance in that game, and all season, built up my determination to make up for it in my senior year. I started practicing the day after the 1955 season ended and I didn't stop. Aside from wanting to help East Bank have a big season in my last year, I was anxious to have a big season myself.

For the first time, then, I realized I was a pretty good basketball player and maybe could be something special. I had become a big man around school and in town, which I enjoyed, because I'd never had any of that. And I knew some colleges were interested in me, which meant I'd probably be able to go to play college ball, which my folks never could have afforded under ordinary circumstances.

Fred Schaus, who was coaching at West Virginia University then, came around to see me and spoke to me about going

to the University, which, of course, had been a dream of
mine. He seemed like a good guy and I admired him as a
coach, so I was kind of walking on air.

Most of our starters were back for the 1956 season. We had
a fairly tall team, we had a year's experience playing as a
team, and we began to play pretty good team ball.

By now I was 6'2" and 165 pounds and a lot stronger than
I had been. I was elected president of the senior class and
it seemed that whenever I opened the newspaper there was a
story about me telling how I was bound to become one of
the great players in state history.

For the first time, then, I had some big pressure on me to
produce, but I didn't mind. I was young and eager and
felt like I could lick the world, on the basketball court, at
least. As a team, we were picked to be third-best in the
country. We turned out to be a lot better than that. We
licked the world—our world, anyway.

I scored 39 points in our first game and averaged 33 points
a game all season. I never scored less than 20 and twice
scored 45, my high school high. There were times that season when I felt I just couldn't miss. Have you ever felt like
that—putting in golf, maybe, or hitting down the line in tennis? It's a beautiful feeling. As a team, we scored 80 or
more points nine times, won a couple of games by 40 points
or so and lost only four games, three of them real close ones.
It's hard to explain the turnabout from the previous season, except that players at the high school level are young and often
mature rapidly, and a poor junior team often becomes an outstanding senior team.

We had won our last four going into the state championship
tournament, and felt we might do pretty well. We got by Seth
in the sectional opener, and then squeezed past DuPont in
the final. For the regionals, we had to go back to Morris
Harvey College, where we had folded so badly the year before,
but now we were very determined. In the first game we drew
St. Albans, a team we had not met during the regular season, but one that had tied us for our conference title. We put

it to them early and won going away. Nitro, a team we had beaten easily during the season, upset Charleston, a team which had beaten us, in the other game, gaining the regional final against us.

Possibly we were overconfident. We played poorly much of the game. At one point, Nitro scored 17 straight points. And they had us by 17 at halftime. We sat in the locker room with our heads hung low and our guts hurting, and coach Williams spoke to us about pride and got us worked up. We could see our high hopes going up in smoke, but we decided we weren't going to just let it go. You can't give up on any game, especially a basketball game. You can get a lot of points in a hurry in basketball. You just never know what'll happen. I've seen teams give up on games, then later realize they could have won with a little more effort. The least you can do is give your best all the way; then even if you lose, you'll still know you did what you could. If you're way behind, maybe you'll lose nine games out of ten, but that tenth one is worth working for.

We went back out on that court against Nitro and began banging the ball in the bucket and chasing them all over the court. They didn't score a basket for the first five minutes of the third period and we began to close in. The crowd, which was only about 2,000, but which was made up mostly of high school kids, who knew how to yell, really began to make noise. I'll never forget it. It was like being on a roller-coaster, just swooping along and picking up momentum. I got 12 points and we got 21 as a team and after three periods, we had closed to within nine.

They started to freeze the ball, then, too early, just like we had done the year before, only this time the situation was a lot different because they already were out of whack. I got a couple of free throws, a tip-in, and a jumper and we got even closer.

There wasn't anything we couldn't do just then. Bob Buckley, who had hurt his ankle, came back in and drove right in for a lay-up. Then Gary Stover drove in for another and we had them by five. At the end, I was dribbling the ball, freezing it, while the Nitro players were desperately trying to get it from me.

We had 'em, 70-65, and the buzzer sounded and I threw the ball up in the air and we came together and began to jump around and hug one another and our crowd came down out of the stands and swept right over us and everyone was laughing and crying and shouting and I'll never forget it as long as I live.

The way they had scheduled it, we still had one game to play the following Friday and had to win it to be one of the four teams in the state finals at the Mountaineer Fieldhouse in Morgantown the following weekend. And it figured to be a tough one, against Huntington East. After a long week of waiting and worrying, it turned out to be as tough as it could be.

We were pretty nervous and we got off real slow. They had us by nine at the quarter and by ten at the half, but we had been this way before. We couldn't help remembering the Nitro game. We sat in the locker room listening to Coach Williams telling us we could come back and we just knew we really could. But they were pretty determined, too. They fought us off all through the third period and had actually built up their lead to eleven points early in the fourth quarter. But we kept banging away and finally they began to crack a little.

They had us by five with a few minutes to play, but they were fading fast. I wanted that ball. I just knew I could put it through the hoop, I got it and drove in for a lay-up to cut the lead to three. I got it again, moved in and shot a jumper and we were within one and that place was a madhouse. Now they had the ball, but I tied up my man, forcing a jump.

Coach Williams signaled for a time-out and told me to slap the ball as far downcourt as I could on the jump and told Jack Landers to break downcourt the minute the ball was thrown up. Now all I had to do was win the jump. But I knew I would.

The buzzer sounded and we went back out on court in some sort of bedlam. The ref threw the ball up and I jumped as high as I could and slapped it way downcourt; Landers grabbed it and broke in on the basket and laid it in. The buzzer went off and we had won, 64-63, and we were hugging one another in happiness once again.

So we were in the state finals. At last, I would get to play on that court, as I'd dreamed of doing, not as a college player —not yet, anyway—but in the finals of the state tournament, which wasn't bad. All we had to do was live through that week in the middle of March 1956.

It wasn't easy. All anyone in our town could talk about was our chances in that tournament. It was all we could think about. And those long days dragged by, one by one, with me feeling like I was going to burst. Everyone was wishing us well and telling me how they were all counting on me, which was something to think about.

I got pretty nervous, I must admit. I was 17 years old and the world was liable to end for me on the coming weekend. I asked my folks to come to the games, which they said they would. They hadn't been to many of my games, and I wanted them there now.

We were not the favorite. Mullens was, and we had to play them in the first game, on Friday night. They had a very tall and very strong team and they had a standout player named Willie Akers, who was a center and who a lot of people thought was better than me. I didn't know, but I was anxious to meet him and prove myself. By then I wanted to be the best. I was closing in on a lot of state scoring records, and everyone kept reminding me of it. But, most of all, I wanted our team to win. We were so close to being state champions it made you feel like crying just to think about not making it.

It was the roughest game I had ever played in. They were as anxious as we were, of course, and they were physically stronger. They belted us pretty good. I was knocked down a number of times. I had guys pushing me and pulling at me all the way. I just hung in there. We all hung tough.

This time, we got off in front. I was real hot and we couldn't miss most of the first half and by intermission we had them by 20. We just walked on air into the locker room and coach tried to deflate us a little, warning us they could come back as we had so many times. We didn't believe him, but he was right. Akers, who scored 27, found the range and they began to whittle away at our lead and before long we were just hanging on. They ran out of time, however, and fell short, 77-73. I'd gotten 43 points and a tourney-record 23 rebounds, but at the buzzer I didn't feel any of us had done so well and I was just relieved we'd gotten by.

Now there was just one more night to get through and one more game to win. That was against Morgantown. We were playing them in their home town and they were not about to go down easy.

We were both real nervous and making a lot of mistakes. At halftime we were dead even and the title was still up in the air. We came out for the second half determined. I guess they were, too, but this was our night. We just took them apart in the third period and got ten points on them. I fouled out with five or six minutes to play, but it was all ours by then. At the finish we were coasting, and at the end we had it, 71-56.

I remember when I walked off the court I felt sort of bad about having fouled out and I had my head down, but I heard noise from that crowd like I'd never heard before. I looked up and the fans were giving me a standing ovation. I couldn't believe it. I was just overwhelmed by it and I cried.

I sat on the bench while the rest of the guys wrapped it up and when it was finally over I raced out on court and jumped around with the rest of them, so happy I just couldn't believe it.

I had scored 39 and become the first player in West Virginia to total more than 900 points in a high school career. I'd averaged more than 33 points a game from start to finish

I was the first West Virginia high school player to score more than 900 points.

and in the last three games of the state tourney had scored 114 points and collected a record 56 rebounds. More important, we were champions. When you're young and everything is important to you, something like this just knocks you out. Out on that court, then, was the happiest moment of my life.

We felt like kings. We went home the next day and were received as though we really were royalty. They threw a parade and made speeches and everyone said how great we were and everyone singled me out and said how great I was, which embarrassed me, but made me proud. I looked at my folks and family and hoped they were proud of me, and

figured they were, which meant something to me. I was someone then, which was something for a lonely, shy kid who
never thought he'd amount to anything. Maybe it wasn't all
so much, but to me it was a great deal.

I went back to that court where I'd practiced alone so
much and shot a few baskets. Having won the championship,
Coach Williams retired from basketball. He also coached football and after winning the championship there, he retired
from that, too. I had a lot ahead of me. But all I knew then
was then. I used to get so excited I could hardly stand it. I
have never again been as excited as I was then. I didn't know
it, but in all the seasons I would play high school and college
and pro basketball, this would be my only real championship. I don't know if knowing that then would have made it
mean more to me. Really, I don't think anything could have.

3
The Recruit

The way college coaches have to recruit high school sports talent is no secret, but it is a questionable practice for all concerned. The coaches woo a lot of the best in hopes of getting a few. They send telegrams, write letters, make telephone calls, put in personal appearances, send others on personal appearances in hopes of interesting promising players in their school, their program, their facilities, their schedule, and the boy's chances of getting to play—getting to play the way he wants to play, and doing well for himself.

I know it's not easy to figure out which things will interest each boy the most. If you represent a top sports school, like Notre Dame in football or UCLA in basketball, for example, you're bound to have a good chance to get good boys. We all want to play with winners, where we'll get attention. If you're not from a top school that's trying to build up, it's kind of tough to get the boys you want.

I'm sure coaches put a lot of time, trouble, and hope into recruiting, and I'm sure they suffer a lot of big disappointments. It may be a game for some, but it's a business for others. College coaches are doing a job. Their livelihoods depend on it. And recruiting is a big part of it. It's one of the things that make college coaching not as attractive as it otherwise might be. It's a hard way to go.

On the other hand, the pressures that are exerted on high school kids are beyond belief. Most of them are just too immature to make wise decisions. Their parents are usually not experienced in this sort of thing and aren't always equipped to give sound advice. The kids are flattered and tempted and turned this way and that.

The school a fellow goes to is very important. If he doesn't get to play or get good coaching or if his team doesn't do well, his chance of playing pro ball are reduced. And if he doesn't get a decent education, his chances of making out all right in life if he doesn't play pro ball are reduced. Many star athletes don't graduate from their colleges. It's tough to give the time you have to give to practicing and playing ball and still do all right in school. And a lot of schools are interested in a boy's studies only so far as keeping him eligible to play is concerned.

I guess I was considered a pretty good prospect, though I wasn't so sure at first. I didn't give much real thought to going to college originally. For one thing, my parents couldn't afford it. For another, I had trouble getting to play, much less starring. As a sophomore at East Bank High, I played a little, then got that broken ankle. All I was thinking of then was making the grade at East Bank, not at any college. In my junior year I came on fast, and people began to talk about my college potential, but practically no one from any colleges showed any interest in me, so I was sort of disappointed and just didn't know what my future might be.

Then it started, at the beginning of my senior season. At first I got a few letters from some small schools. They were interested in my playing basketball for them and invited me to visit their campuses whenever I wished. Of course, I got excited, and if I could have signed up with one of them right then and there, I just might have done it.

But then as the season wore on, more letters came and from bigger schools. Pretty soon, whenever I'd do something good, I'd get telegrams of congratulations as well as letters.

Then the phone calls started coming in. Then alumni, assistant coaches, head coaches, star players started coming around to see me. Wherever I went, people were touting me on their place. It got to be ridiculous. Once I came home and three different coaches were waiting for me on my front porch. I was 17 years old and I didn't know what to say to them or how to handle them.

Near the end of the season, it was obvious I was a real good prospect. And I had above a B average, which was extra important because it meant almost any school could get me in without any trouble and could probably keep me eligible without any trouble. The pressure built and built and built and it's kind of amazing, looking back on it, that I was able to play as well as I did.

By the end of the season, I'd guess I had about sixty scholarship offers, plus some more from some of the junior colleges. I heard from just about every school in the South. I heard from a lot of the top schools in the East and Midwest. And I heard some from schools in the Far West. I guess some guys have had more, but I felt like I had plenty. It's not too hard to choose from two or three schools, but it's pretty tough to pick from sixty. Of course a lot of them just didn't interest me for one reason or another, but a lot did.

As I've said, it was always my ambition to play for my home state university. I always followed the West Virginia University basketball games, saw a few, and always dreamed of playing there. The school was close to home. The coach, Fred Schaus, had built a big winning record, he had been one of the first to approach me, and he seemed to me to be a very nice, sincere sort of person. My Dad didn't interfere too much, but Mom liked the school, liked Fred, and liked the thought of my not going too far away, so she made it clear she hoped I'd go there.

But it's a funny thing, Schaus didn't seem all that excited about me. Maybe he was just using the soft-sell approach, but I got the idea I wasn't all that important to him. I went to a

When West Virginia Coach Fred Schaus was recruiting, he didn't seem all that excited about me.

football game there and no one paid too much attention to me They had a lot of big boys to play basketball, and I didn't think they needed me that much. They seemed more interested in Willie Akers. Willie and Butch Goode and I had played basketball together at summer camp and we had made a kind of pledge to all go to the same school. I don't know how set we were on sticking to it, but we were all having the same problem, making up our minds. We did say we'd talk it over before making our final choice.

I visited a lot of campuses. A lot of them were real nice. And the people were too. Some of the coaches practically guaranteed national championships and All-American honors if I went to their schools.

I'm not going to name the schools, but some of the offers went way, way beyond what the NCAA permits. One school offered to pay me $300 a month during the school year, $250 a week during the summer, a free car, all the clothes

I wanted free, and four free round-trip plane flights home a year. Another offered me a thousand dollars a week during the summer, the free clothes and car and plane flights, which I guess are sort of standard, and practically promised I'd get to marry a rich girl and so never have to worry about money the rest of my life. This was ridiculous, I know, but that was it and they seemed serious about it. Of course, I never took them up on any of it, so I don't know if they'd have come across or if it was just talk, but I do know a lot of people got a lot to play ball in college.

I'd be lying if I said I wasn't tempted. I hadn't had a whole lot, so I was tempted all right. But I was warned that if I got caught taking more than I should, my career might be ruined, so I was scared, too. And I wasn't brought up to do the wrong thing and I knew it wouldn't sit right with me, so I was sort of turned against it, too. Still, illegal or not, these offers showed how much some schools wanted me, and I had to be flattered by that.

Of all the things that happened to me in that period, I remember most vividly a meeting I had with a coach after I scored 39 points in an all-star game. He invited me to his hotel room. I wasn't really interested, but he pleaded, so I went.

He had built a big name doing well at an Eastern school for a lot of years and he was having trouble continuing his success at a Southwest Conference school. He said he needed me in the worst possible way. He practically begged me to sign with his school. He wound up crying.

That really shook me. Here was a grown man, a famous man in basketball, begging me, crying over me. For the first time then I began to realize how much my basketball ability might mean and how important I could be to some people.

When the state finals were held in Morgantown, the University assigned athletes to host the players. Hot Rod Hundley, just about the biggest name the Mountaineers had ever had and headed for a pro career with the Lakers, was as-

signed to me, which was pretty impressive and pretty flattering. Maybe I was naive, but I thought he was genuinely interested in me as a person.

He was sort of sophisticated, a swinger, a fun-loving guy,
which he still is, and which impressed me, though I'm not
cut that way. He told me he'd paid off half the fieldhouse and
it was up to me to go to the university and pay off the other
half. I've learned since that he also told Schaus he thought
I was a better prospect than Willie Akers, which Schaus has
admitted he didn't think at the time, and Schaus respected
Rod's judgment of players, which always has been good.

In time, I decided Fred really did think highly of me. He
said things like I was the best player in West Virginia high
school circles and if he got me he'd just put me on the court
and throw me the ball and we'd win, which, if just talk, was
still nice to hear.

I was tempted to go to other schools, like Texas A&M and
Maryland, especially Maryland. I don't know why Maryland,
since it's never been big in basketball, but I thought the campus was beautiful and I liked the people I met there and the
way they treated me. Now people say if I'd gone to Maryland,
as I seriously thought about doing, I'd have started a whole
basketball tradition. Maybe. And maybe I wouldn't have done
well there and the team wouldn't have done well and nothing
would have worked out for me the way it did. Who knows?

But I know West Virginia University was always first on
my list, right from when I was a boy. I swear that they only
offered me and only gave me what was permitted, which was
free tuition and books, free room and board, thirty-five dollars a month spending money, and fifteen dollars a month
laundry money. But by then, I just wanted to be done with
all the big talk and the traveling around and the being
hounded and I wanted to go where I'd wanted to go all along,
where I thought I'd be comfortable, where the people seemed
sincere and didn't make all sorts of phony-sounding promises.
And once I decided, I felt like I'd done the right thing.

The newspapers had been making a fuss over where I'd go and the Charleston papers were pleased. I called Willie Akers up and apologized for announcing it without conferring with him, but I said I just couldn't take it any more. And he and Goode did decide to go to the University with me, too.

It was a big thing for a West Virginia boy to go to play basketball at West Virginia University. We didn't have any pro sports teams and we weren't big-time in many things, but we were proud of our University basketball. The school had had four All-Americans—Scotty Hamilton, Leland Byrd, Mark Workman, and Rod Hundley—and a lot of other fine players like Fred Schaus, Lloyd Sharrar, Jimmy Walthall, Eddie Beach, and Jim Sottile. Schaus, who played pro ball in Fort Wayne and New York, had returned to coach and in his first two years had won the school's first two Southern Conference titles, had gone unbeaten in the conference, and had won 40 out of 60 games overall. He was only 32 and was building the Mountaineers up nationally.

The school had an enrollment of only around 6,000 students on campus, and the Mountaineer Field House, located alongside the football stadium and the Monongahela River, was 30 days old and wasn't always filled to its 6,800-seat capacity.

I can't say I was happy there right from the start. I don't guess many kids are happy in college at first. For a lot like me it means being away from home for the first time in our lives, among strangers, in strange surroundings, with all sorts of new pressures on us. I was a small-town boy and I was pretty homesick, and considered quitting and going home.

Fred Schaus says this is typical and that the crucial point comes in the first few months of college life before Christmas vacation. Up to then, kids miss their friends and everything else back home. But when they get home, they usually find their friends are doing new things, a lot has changed, and it's no longer the way it was. People talk to them about the college and the kids talk up the college and pretty soon they miss it and are anxious to get back. Once they go back, they're usually all right, which is the way it was for me.

I lived in a dormitory my freshman year. Then, in my sophomore year, I took a small apartment off campus with Willie Akers and Joe Posch. And in my junior and senior years, we moved in with the Dinardi sisters, Ann and Erlinda.

This may sound strange, but it was strictly straight. They are practically institutions at the University—elderly ladies, very nice, very keen on sports, and very fond of athletes. Their house is near the fieldhouse and they almost always had athletes living with them, getting mothered by them. We were mostly a lazy, sloppy bunch, and we needed them. We also needed decent food now and then. That training-food table at the University, which is supposed to be so great, was just terrible. I had lived with the Dinardi sisters the summer before I started college and I finished up with them and they helped me through.

When I got to be prominent on campus as an athlete, I got to be in demand, but I didn't go for much of that. I was talked into running for president of the senior class, but then I withdrew, which caused some talk. The fact was I realized I was being run only because I was a big sports hero and I didn't care much for that. I didn't think I'd be a good man for the job and I didn't have the time to put into it that it deserved, so I thought better of it and pulled out.

There have been some misconceptions about my life in West Virginia, at home and at the University. There was one major magazine story which made me and my family sound like a bunch of poor hillbillies, which was not true, and made me seem like the most unpopular man on campus, which was not true. It is impossible for a basketball star not to be popular, deserved or not.

Some people thought I was stuck up and some branded me as something of a hermit, but this was just because I've never been a good mixer. I've always liked to be by myself a lot, and I've never been outgoing.

I wasn't wild about school work. I majored in phys ed and studied enough to get by, but I didn't have any idea what I wanted to do with my life. I saved up enough working one summer to buy my first car, a two year old Pontiac, but I didn't go anywhere.

The University had something of a reputation of being a fun place and it deserved some of this, at least while I was there. You could have a good time there, especially if you were a sports star, but my idea of a good time was a movie or an evening at the pool hall, which is not everyone's idea of a good time.

I didn't accept any invitations to join any fraternities and I steered clear of the campus hangouts. I treated everyone as nice as I could and I was treated nicely by everyone and I don't think I really offended anyone, but I just wasn't much of a swinger, and I went my own way, doing my own things. I was close to my roomies and some of the other ball players, and I found a girl.

Her name was Martha Jane Kane, and I think what I liked about her best at first was that she didn't know I was a basketball star when we first met. And very early in life it became important to me to be taken for myself, not for a basketball star, proud as I've always been about my basketball ability.

You only spend a couple of hours a day on the basketball court, and your life extends far beyond that. Everything I have in life I have gotten mainly through basketball, and no one could be more dedicated to his profession than I have been to basketball, but I am more than just a basketball player; I am whatever I am inside of me, where I live, and I get hungry sometimes to be considered as just a person, with ideas and feelings about life that have nothing to do with sports. More than anything I wanted to be considered as just a person at the University, where, as at most universities, athletes are tin gods, something to be admired, but not touched.

Jane was from Weston, West Virginia, from a good family. As I've said, I had only a couple of dates in high school and I had only a couple in college until I met Jane. I was real shy, but I liked her on sight. After watching her a while, I got up the nerve to arrange a date with her through a friend. After I took her out a couple of times, I found I was relaxed in her company. I think it was on the second date that I spoke to her for the first time, which was pretty fast work for me. Which is an exaggeration, but not much. But I always felt comfortable with Jane.

It's hard to explain, except maybe there are people who are right for each other, and I always felt right with Jane. I didn't have to pretend anything with her. I didn't have to try to be anything I wasn't. I'm not the easiest guy in the world to get along with. I'm very demanding, mainly of myself, very self-critical, never really satisfied, very moody, very quiet, sort of a loner. Jane understood me then and she understands me now.

Her folks weren't all that keen on me at first. Her father had an idea athletes led a hard life and died of heart attacks at the age of 30. But they warmed to me. And Jane was all for me. We went together part of the time I was in school and got married late in my senior year. Now we have three sons.

The Athletic Department arranged jobs for me while I was at West Virginia—if you can call them jobs. Some of them were not too tough. That much they did do for me, and I did need the little money I could pick up. Even before I got there, after I graduated from high school, they got me a job with a labor gang at Charleston. I dug ditches and cleaned up the place, but not very well. They made me a safety inspector but the boss said he should fire me because I was a safety hazard. I used to go fishing all the time. The thing I remember most is that I tried to chew tobacco, which all the guys did because they would get too thirsty. Oh boy, did I get sick! I lay under a tree and died. Then I never tried that again.

One of my summer jobs during college was "public relations" and playing basketball for a Charleston dairy.

One summer I worked for a Charleston dairy, doing public relations work and playing for the plant basketball team. Another summer I sold license plates at the Department of Motor Vehicles. Willie Akers worked there, too. Our bookkeeping left something to be desired. They may still be trying to straighten it out.

I worked in a Charleston clothing store part-time, which is where I picked up my unusual taste in clothes, to which Elgin Baylor will attest. For a while I had a job watching the football field. Another time I had a job watching the tennis courts. I never saw anyone at either place.

My main job was playing basketball.

Kentucky won the NCAA championship in 1957-58, but we still beat them that season in the Kentucky Invitation Tournament. UPI

4
The Mountaineer

Playing basketball can be a full-time job in college. Basketball was king at West Virginia. We had a good all-around sports program, from football to gymnastics, but basketball was king. The athletic director, Robert "Red" Brown, had been basketball coach for four years before moving up in 1954. He had developed freewheeling, high-scoring teams, which brought the school national ranking. He had coached one All-American, Mark Workman, and recruited another, Rod Hundley. When Schaus became coach in 1955, he continued the school's rise as a national power. He inherited Hundley, recruited Lloyd Sharrar, and won the school's first two Southern Conference championships in his first two years.

My freshman year was the 1956-57 season. It was Hundley's last year. He set most of the school scoring records, including 54 points for one game, 798 points for one season, and 2,180 points for his career, and he had done it in such a showy way that he was bound to be missed, not only as an effective player, but also as a colorful performer. With Sharrar, a six-ten center, helping out, the varsity had one of the best seasons the school ever had. They were a quick team, which shot well. They won 25 of 30 games and were ranked seventh nationally in the final Associated Press poll, although they then lost to Canisius in the first game of the NCAA championship tournament.

41

My freshman team won all 17 games it played. Quentin Barnette was our coach and we had a good club. I had Akers, Goode, Jim Ritchie, Jim Warren, and Jim Reiss as team-mates. Reiss later transferred to NYU, where he was to prove a thorn in our side three seasons later.

Many of our games were against schools whose names didn't exactly strike terror in our hearts. But many of them were close. For example, we beat Potomac State by one point, West Virginia Wesleyan by two points, West Virginia Tech reserves by two points, and Greenbrier Military by three points. And we had romps over such as Alderson Broaddus, Wheeling, and Bluefield.

But a lot of these were varsity teams, playing seniors and juniors, while we were all freshmen playing together for the first time, so few of these were soft touches for us. And we did win and kept winning and got toughened winning close games. We also got toughened scrimmaging the varsity some, and I think we proved we were a good team when we played a special game against the varsity before some 4,000 students and lost by only four points.

I led the freshmen with averages of 19 points and 17 rebounds a game. Still, I didn't feel I was very good. I had a good shooting percentage, but I didn't feel I shot well and so I didn't shoot a whole lot. At 6-3 I was tall enough on that level of competition and although I only weighed about 165 pounds, I was a good jumper and I wasn't afraid, so I did all right off the boards. I worked hard on my all-around game, on ballhandling, which was not my best thing, and on defense, which was fairly good.

I wasn't fully settled in at school yet, I wasn't happy, and so I wasn't able to really let loose. I didn't exactly feel indispensable, which is something I guess I need. As a freshman, if I didn't do it, someone else did. If I played a bad game, we won anyway. I wasn't too inspired.

As a sophomore I moved up to the varsity and was initiated into Mountaineer spirit. Schaus believed that school spirit and team spirit are a big part of winning. And they are. They carry you over hard times and help you to keep going and to fight from behind, and this is something every player and every team doesn't have.

Schaus insisted that we take pride in our school and our winning tradition. He said he wanted us to start by looking better than anyone else. To give you an odd example, he insisted we all shave our armpits. He got us a fancy gold and blue ball to warm up with and then a 90-foot gold and blue carpet, over which we ran onto the court before each game. The idea was that everyone, including us, was to feel that we were something special.

We were, too, in my sophomore season. Schaus was a good coach—friendly, rather than tough—who stressed an aggressive, wide-open style of play, more than conservative, fundamental basketball, and he had the sort of talent to make this style work.

Sharrar was back, along with Bob Smith, a good forward, and Don Vincent and Jody Gardner, a couple of quick guards. There were some experienced reserves, such as Bob Clousson, Bucky Bolyard, and Jay Jacobs, and the best of us from our fine freshman team of the preceding season—myself, Akers, and Goode.

I think, taking it at its level of competition, this was the finest team I ever played on. We had a big man and a lot of speed. We played tough defense, pressing a lot and stealing the ball a lot. And we shot so well we wound up second in the nation in shooting. Perhaps most important, we played as a team.

I had a good season myself, but not an outstanding one. Frankly, I think it was one of the two hardest seasons I've ever gotten through in basketball. The only other one to compare with it would be my first year as a pro, later on. In both cases, the main problem was adjusting to a faster level of competition and gaining confidence. For the first time, I was playing with and against guys who were just as good as

I was. The difference between the competition I'd faced before college and the competition I now faced was like the difference between night and day.

I'm not saying the Southern Conference played the toughest basketball you could find anywhere. It didn't and it doesn't. Very few nationally rated teams come out of the Southern Conference, and we seldom lost a game in the conference all the years I was in school. But there were some teams which had good players and were often hard to beat, especially when we had to play them on the road, because a lot of the schools in this conference had old fieldhouses, which were cramped and dark and hard on visitors who weren't used to them. And we always played some of the best teams in the country outside of the conference, often on the road, in the big cities, such as New York and Chicago and Philadelphia, usually before large, loud crowds. I was a small-town boy, only 19 years old, and I just wasn't used to the sort of pressure I got.

I didn't play badly. I shot and rebounded fairly well, and I had a quickness which helped me on defense, but I made a lot of mistakes. I worked hard and improved steadily all season, but I had a lot of adjustments to make as I went along. I was the only sophomore who won a starting spot, but after only three games, Coach Schaus called me into the office to lecture me.

I remember very vividly him saying, "Jerry, I don't know if we're gonna' be able to keep starting you. You've got to give us more scoring and more rebounding or I may have to sit you down awhile. Maybe you're not ready yet. I'll decide off your performance in the next few games."

I hadn't scored much, but I felt I'd been doing a fair all-around job and others seemed to feel so and I just couldn't believe a coach could run out of patience with a player so quickly, so I figured Schaus wasn't serious and was just trying to light a fire under me. But maybe he really felt that way. You never can tell. And once a coach gets down on you, you may never again get the sort of chances you deserve. So

I grit my teeth and determined to bear down harder. During the remainder of my college career, I was never again threatened with demotion.

It's funny, but while I'm very critical of myself, inside, I don't take too kindly from criticism from outside. It's a failing, I guess, and I try not to show it. It's just that I'm thin-skinned and easily hurt. I've deserved criticism lots of times, but I respond better to encouragement.

After the session with Schaus, I was down in the dumps and, despite my determination to show him, I only got 14 points and then 15 points as we won two more games. Then I turned the bend. I got hot and scored 28 as we beat Richmond, 76-74, in overtime. I got the ball and shot a basket with just 12 seconds to play that sent the game into overtime, then scored seven points in the overtime, including the basket that won it with only three seconds left.

Coming through in the clutch like that, I got to feeling good about myself again, and we got to feeling good as a team. We also gained some savvy. Maybe Richmond wasn't really such a tough team, but they played us tough and we had all we could do to win. We realized we couldn't hold anyone lightly.

After six straight wins, we now were faced with our first real challenge. It was the Christmas holiday period and we were booked into the Kentucky Invitational Classic at the Lexington Memorial Coliseum, the home grounds of the University of Kentucky. We were one of four teams in it, and Adolph Rupp's Kentucky Wildcats were heavily favored.

They deserved to be. He's a tough old coach and as usual he had a tough team, a quick, well-disciplined team which eventually would go on to win the NCAA championship that year. And they almost never lost at home. So we drew them in the first game. But we were sharp that night, and we beat them without too much trouble, 77-70.

In the finals, we stayed sharp, and with Akers scoring nine straight points at one point, we took North Carolina even more easily, 75-64. We couldn't wait to go home. In Morgantown, we received a big reception. We were rated in the top three in the country and people were beginning to talk about us as possible national champs. In my first year of college ball, I was a bit overwhelmed by such thoughts.

We won a couple more, then a big one in Philadelphia's Palestra against a strong Villanova club. Here we had to play before a crowd of around 8,000 fans. We'd played for crowds of more than 10,000 in Lexington, and they were rabid, but not the way they are in the Palestra. Philadelphia has a strong local circuit of college basketball teams, including Villanova, LaSalle, St. Joseph's, and Temple; they bring in top visitors and they follow college basketball more enthusiastically than they do anywhere outside of New York. In New York's Madison Square Garden crowds of 18,000 or more are not uncommon, but they're sort of neutral. They root for the home side, but they look forward to seeing well-publicized visitors. They want them to do well and treat them with respect if they do. In Philadelphia they just want to beat you. The fans set up a great racket, and it's all in favor of the home clubs.

They were raising the roof most of the game because Villanova was taking us apart. In fact, they had us by 14 with about eight minutes to play. Then we began to come. I got hot and the guys began to feed me. I scored 17 of my team's last 23 points. In the last 40 seconds I scored two baskets and fed Sharrar for the game-winner with just two seconds to go. We won, 76-75, and I wound up with 37, which turned out to be the high mark of my sophomore season. It was a high point of the season for all of us. Coming from behind to beat a good team in that place with everyone against us made us feel like maybe we weren't ever going to lose.

We won three more for 14 straight, which was, I think, the longest streak the school ever had. My teams had 40 straight, over three seasons, counting the last nine in high school ball, the 17 as a college freshman, and these 14. Maybe

I'm lucky to have quickness, which helps me on defense, like here
when I blocked a shot by George Marshall of George Washington.
CHARLESTON DAILY MAIL

we were all overconfident. Or maybe you just can't win them all, which is no secret. We went into Durham, North Carolina, and got beat by Duke, 72-68. It was no disgrace.

We had an easy game next out, against Florida State, and poured it on, 103-51, one of seven games that season in which we scored 100 or more points. We wound up winning our last nine games of the regular season and went into New York's Madison Square Garden, where we beat St. John's, 87-78. I got 21 and Don Vincent got 17 and we played well. You always want to do well in New York and we especially wanted to do well because we wanted to hang on to our high national ranking.

New York is the big town and a lot of publicity comes from there. Most athletes feel they have to prove themselves there. It's a very special place for athletes. It's particularly special for basketball players, because the Garden has long been a home for basketball.

At Penn State we got off slow and trailed by 10 at halftime, but that didn't discourage us because we were used to coming from behind. I scored 21 in the second half and we won 74-71. Then in the last game of the regular season, we beat George Washington, 113-107, in double overtime. That was in the Uline Arena in Washington, D.C., which has to be the single worst court I've ever played on. We wound up the regular season with a 21-1 record, the best the school ever had, and we were ranked first nationally, in both the Associated Press and United Press polls, for the first time in the school's history.

For the second straight season we had gone undefeated in Southern Conference games and had stretched our winning streak in the conference to 28 straight games, but the way they work it there we now had to win the conference post-season tournament to win the conference championship and a berth in the NCAA tournament.

It's stupid. You can't play everyone in the country during the season, so a national tournament is the only way to decide the national championship, even if the best team may not always win. You can play everyone in your conference during the season, but why bother if you're going to throw the results away and settle it in a three-night tournament later? It's just not right. The champion should be the team that proved itself over the long season. Maybe the best team will usually win the tournament, but not always. It's not sour grapes on my part. We won three straight games and the tournament easily that year, and we won the tournament every year I was in school. But a pretty good Davidson team that was nationally ranked and dominated the conference all season got knocked out of the post-season tournament a few years ago, and it didn't seem fair to me.

Probably I feel strong about it because we did lose to a weaker team in the first game of the NCAA tournament. We lost, 89-84, to Manhattan in the Garden in New York. It was a terrible shock and all these years later I can still hardly believe it. Manhattan has had some good teams, but they weren't anything special that year and they didn't go anywhere after they beat us. We never had a thought we could lose to them, but we did. We were overconfident. We had proved all season we weren't a choke-up team, but when we got behind this time with all that was at stake, we tensed up. I got stuck with four personal fouls in the first half and wound up with only ten points in the game, which was awful and which let the team down. Everyone now says that I'm some sort of great clutch player, but there are nights when I sure wasn't and this was one of them.

We had a better ball club than they did. If we'd have played them again the next night, we'd have beaten them by 20 points, but we didn't get to play them the next night. If we played them 100 times, we'd have beaten them 99 times, but this was the hundredth time. They played better and so they deserved to win, but it was the biggest disappointment I'd had in my career until then. It taught me a valuable lesson: you have to try harder against the teams that aren't as good. It's easy to get ready for the great clubs. It takes a special sort of discipline to get up for the weaker teams. And every club gets upset by a weaker team once in a while. That's what an upset is. The real champs just simply don't let it happen very often.

So we wound up 26-2. It was sort of sad when we saw a Kentucky team which we had beaten decisively over the holidays go on to the national title. I really think we had the best college team in the country that year, but we didn't prove it on the court, which is the only place that counts. All we could do was wait for next year.

I'd scored 498 points, averaging just under 18 points a game. I'd begun to get some national publicity and was being touted for stardom. I couldn't help thinking that maybe I could make All-American. That's sort of a dream of every kid, I think. I felt like I was ready to prove myself and I figured if we had a good season, I just might make it.

And 1958-59 did come. We did have a good season. Our record wasn't as good as the year before, but we went further with it. And I did make All-American. I became a key man on the team and I responded to that sort of challenge. I think I always need that to do my best. I have to feel everyone is looking to me. I shot a lot and shot well, and when we needed a basket, I wanted the shot and often made it. I was maturing physically, gaining a little weight and strength, which helped me off the boards. I've always been quick, which makes up for any mistakes I make on defense. I gamble a lot and get beat a lot, but I can usually cover up. I began to steal the ball a lot and to block a lot of shots that year. I worked real hard at both ends of the court. I was not a finished player, but I was becoming a good one.

I would not even begin to repeat what was beginning to be said and written about me. Other players, coaches, writers were beginning to say I was the greatest this or that. I wasn't, but I wasn't going to argue with anyone about it. I don't like to say good things about myself, but I don't mind if other people say good things about me. I may deny it, but I'll like it inside. I don't think the man's been born with so little ego he doesn't enjoy praise, and the sort of praise I began to get then and have gotten ever since has always made me proud inside. And it's always made me play better. I have a great deal to live up to.

I had help. You don't do much without help. We had a good team. Big Lloyd Sharrar was gone, so we were a lot smaller than we'd been, and when we had trouble or got beat, it was usually off the boards. But if we were small we were again a very quick club, tough on defensive, pressing a lot and staying on top of the other clubs. And we were a good shooting team again, ranking second nationally in shooting for the second straight season. And we were a club with a lot of guts. We trailed at halftime 13 times that season and won nine of the games.

Our soft spot was center. A senior, Bob Clousson, and a sophomore, Jim Ritchie, shared the spot. My old buddy Akers moved up to team with me up front. Bob Smith and Bucky Bolyard teamed in the backcourt. The bench was strong.

We were very inconsistent in the first part of the season. We won our first four, including a 101-63 drubbing of Duke, which was revenge for the only loss we had suffered during the previous regular season. Then Virginia came to town and set us on our ear, 75-72. It wasn't a Southern Conference game, but a loss is a loss. You just can't take any team lightly. It's easy to say you learn lessons, but they don't always stick.

We went to the Kentucky holiday tourney as defending champs and won our first game against Oklahoma State, but lost the title game to Kentucky, 97-91. A lot was made in advance of the duel I'd have with All-American candidate Johnny Cox and I won it, 36-16, but we lost and the standing-room-only crowd of 11,700 in Lexington was happy.

Let down, we then went into Chicago Stadium and got knocked off by Northwestern in double overtime, 118-109. I had one of the worst games I ever had in college. If I'd been flying over the middle of the ocean, I couldn't have dropped a ball and gotten it wet. I scored just 17.

At this point, we had played 10 games and lost three. The last game of 1958 was the turning point of our season. It was against Tennessee in Knoxville. They were more like a football team than a basketball team, but we fought back. I didn't shoot much, but I didn't miss much either. I hit 17 out of 25 shots from the field and 10 of 11 from the foul line and got 44 points, which was to be the most I'd ever score in a single college game, and we pulled it out, 76-72. I guess the chemistry was right. If you could put your finger on what you do different on nights like this, you'd do it all the time. You can't, so you don't.

So we were in the new year, 1959, and, as it turned out, we were off on a hot streak. We won our next eight, including an overtime game at Penn State and a two-pointer at home with Western Kentucky. However, going into an important game, the first game ever to be televised nationally out of Morgantown, against Holy Cross, Schaus was concerned about the way I had been playing. He called me into his office for a pep talk.

I admitted that I'd been brooding over our two straight losses to Kentucky and Northwestern. He said, "I don't want any losers on this team, but you have to put losses aside and bounce back from them. You can't hold yourself accountable for everything that happens to this team, not the defeats, and not the victories either. You get down on yourself too easily. You've been playing well, but not as well as you can. When you loosen up, you'll really be something."

Looking back on it, I think his talk helped me some—if not then, later on. I remember it, so it must have had an impact on me. You can't take everything on yourself in team games and you have to ride out the ups and downs.

We started slowly against Holy Cross and were down by 13 at halftime. We sat in the locker room sucking on lemons listening to Schaus tell us how the whole country was watching us. Then we went out and I got 23 in the second half and we won by six, 96-90. Then we went into New York and lost to NYU in two overtime periods, 72-70. Tom Sanders, who later plagued my pro teams when he joined Boston, wrapped us up in his long arms that night. I felt we had a better team and we played a pretty good game, but they played a better game. Somehow we never seemed to play our best in the Garden, maybe because we wanted to so much.

We won our last four games of the regular season and finished at 22-4, which was fine, really, if not as good as the season before. We had stretched our undefeated string in conference games to 41 straight, but we still had to win the conference tournament in Richmond to get into the NCAA playoffs.

In the opener, we beat Davidson easily. In the semis, we just barely got past William & Mary, 85-82. I didn't lead this victory; Lee Patrone did. I scored 38 points in 35 minutes, but fouled out when they had us by four. Patrone came barreling in off the bench and scored three baskets and assisted on a fourth as we came from behind.

In the final, we routed The Citadel. This was one of my best games. I got 27 points, 19 rebounds, six assists, and held Art Musselman, who had been scoring a bundle, to seven points. Again, Patrone came off the bench to help. He played only 56 minutes in that tournament, but scored 54 points. That's the kind of help you need from your bench.

So, we were in the NCAA tourney again, though not the favorites as we had been the year before. Kansas State, California, and Cincinnati were regarded as the best teams in the nation. We were rated only number ten. Our record was better than that. We deserved to have been ranked higher. But we had to prove it now. Kansas State had Bob Boozer, Cal had Darrall Imhoff, and Cincy had Oscar Robertson. All

We almost never lost a home game. Here I am driving against Penn State's Hancock en route to a victory in 1957-58. UPI

had been named All-American unanimously, as I also had been.

Back in New York's Garden, where we had been upset out of the tournament by Manhattan the year before and where we had been upset by NYU this season, we drew Dartmouth as our first opponent. It was part of a triple-header which drew almost 15,000 fans. Dartmouth had a good Ivy League team and a fine individual player in Rudy LaRusso, who would later be my teammate with the Lakers and a solid NBA star. But Willie Akers covered him effectively and we won easily.

We went back down south to Charlotte for the regionals. We just couldn't seem to get untracked against St. Joseph's of Philadelphia. Schaus poured it on at halftime, but it didn't seem to change anything. With 13 minutes left, we were 18 points behind. In desperation, Schaus had moved me into the pivot. I scored 14 points in less than four minutes. I kept getting the ball and putting it up and it kept going in.

With one minute to go we had gotten to within a point of them and they were in a panic and the fans were in an uproar. I stole the ball and drove in and laid it home to put us ahead with 25 seconds to play and the whole world going crazy. I got the ball again and got fouled. I walked up to the free throw line and tried not to think of anything but the ball and the basket. I knew we needed the points. I got both of them and that sewed it up because only three seconds were left. I wound up with 36 points and we wound up with three more points than they had, 95-92. It was one of the great nights.

Then we had to calm down for the regional finals. We faced Boston University, but they weren't in our class. Still they had us even at halftime. I got 20 in the second half and we won, 86-82.

Now we were one of four teams left in the running for the national championships and it was on to the NCAA finals in big old Freedom Hall in Louisville the following weekend, along with a hometown team, Louisville, and California and Cincinnati. Cincy's Oscar Robertson and I were considered the two best college players in the country and there were a lot of arguments as to which of us was best. Everyone was hoping we would meet face to face in the final, but it wasn't to be.

California eliminated Cincinnati on Friday night. We eliminated Louisville. Despite the support of the hometown crowd of more than 18,000, Louisville wasn't equal to us. We wiped them out, 94-79. I got 27 points in the first half and we pulled far ahead. I took only six shots and fed off a lot in the second half. I wound up with 38 points and 15 rebounds. They had a good team, but we didn't play a better game all year. I wished we'd saved some of it for the next night.

Another capacity crowd turned out for the final. I thought we would win. If we'd started better, we might have. We got off to a bad start. I think it was a matter of styles. They had a well-coached, sound defensive club built around the big center, Imhoff, who later became my Laker teammate in the NBA. At that time he was a very good player, who was effective in college ball in his team's pattern of play. He was much bigger than anyone we had and he dominated the boards. They played careful, conservative, possession ball. We had a run-and-shoot team and they contained our fast break. We missed some shots early and began to press.

We were far behind before we began to straighten ourselves out. I had picked up four personal fouls and had been benched for a brief time, but time was running out and Schaus had to use me. One more foul and I'd be out. And we had to go into an all-court pressing defense to get the ball as often as possible. I had nothing to lose, so I went all out. It was gambling strategy, but when what you're doing isn't working, you have to do something else. We went after them. Amazingly, this well-disciplined Cal team began to crack a little bit. I guess it was the high stakes. They lost their momentum. We began to disrupt their ballhandling and started closing in.

We crept closer and closer. The noise in the arena was overwhelming. I was weary, bruised, soaked with sweat, but I didn't even realize it. Suddenly, I felt we were going to pull out another great, dramatic victory. I had the ball in my hands and was ready to go for the winning basket when the buzzer sounded. It was too late to get off a shot and we had no great, dramatic victory. We had been beaten by a single point, 71-70.

I totaled 28 points and 11 rebounds in that final game. I had led all scorers and rebounders in every tournament game and had tied the NCAA five-game tournament record of 160 points. In the voting for the Most Valuable Player in the tourney, I received 45 votes, Imhoff seven, Oscar three, and Denny Fitzpatrick of Cal one. I had much that I was and am proud of, but I would have swapped it all to have won that tournament.

It was hard to stay on the court for the post-game ceremonies. It was hard to watch Cal get the big trophy. I felt we were a better team. I don't always feel that when we lose, really. Years later, I didn't feel that when my Laker teams lost pro playoffs to Boston. They were better than we were. But I think if we'd have played Cal the next night, we'd have beaten them. In sports there isn't always a next night. You do it when your time comes, or you don't do it.

I found it hard to take my trophy, though the cheering of the crowd was something to hear, and sent chills down my spine. It was hard not to cry. I wasn't too proud to cry. I mean, what good are the fancy records and the high honors if you lose the championship by one point? I wouldn't ever want to play badly in any game or any tournament, but I'd rather have just played fair and had Imhoff or Oscar get the records and the laurels and have had my team get the title. I can't imagine anyone feeling otherwise. You play to win. That's it. Losing that one was a deep disappointment to me and the hurt of it has never left me. I don't think it ever will.

I wound up with 903 points that season, surpassing Rod Hundley's one-season school record. My shooting percentage from the field was the best I'd ever have, just under 52 percent. I also had almost 100 assists and led the team with more than 400 rebounds. My all-around play had improved a lot, though I wasn't about to dribble my way onto the Harlem Globetrotters. I was voted the Roger Hicks Memorial Trophy, which is given to the team MVP in memory of a member of the Mountaineers' 1942 National Invitational Tournament champions who was killed in World War II. I was also named Basketball Player of the Year and Athlete of the Year in the conference. Schaus was named Coach of the Year for the second straight season.

This was not the end of the season, however. The Pan-American Games were to be played in Chicago that summer of 1959 and Schaus was named coach of the U.S. basketball entry. I was selected for the squad, along with Oscar Robertson and many of the other top amateurs. I always thought it would be fun to play against teams from other countries with other styles and I looked forward to the experience. It was quite an experience, too, though it wasn't good on all counts. Attendance at the Games was poor, and the quality of our opposition was poor.

We scored more than 100 points in beating Cuba, Mexico, and El Salvador very easily. We also beat Mexico, Puerto Rico, and Canada without much trouble. We did have one tough game. A big Brazilian team slowed the game on us, did well off the boards, and almost upset us. We were lucky to take them by two points, 45-43. But we did finish undefeated and did get our gold medals. And it is a special sort of thrill to represent your country, to know you have played and won not just for yourself and not just for a team, but for the U.S.A. It brings out some kind of patriotism that many of us don't realize we have.

5
From Campus to Olympus

I had dreamed of taking part in the Olympic Games. It was always a distant dream, vague and sort of unreal, as though I did not think it would happen. But at the end of my senior year, in the summer of 1960, the Olympics would be held in Rome, and I knew I had a good chance of being chosen for the U.S. team. Having had a taste of international competition, I eagerly looked forward to the glamorous games.

After that I expected to turn pro.

I had proven myself in fast company. I had established myself as a star, everyone was talking about my pro potential, and it was not unreasonable for me to expect to make the pros, possibly as a star. I had begun to see that basketball, a game I love, could be and probably would be my future for a long time to come, and probably a very good one for Jane and myself. We were talking marriage. I'd gained a lot of confidence and poise. There is nothing like success for doing that.

The success I wanted first, however, was the NCAA championship, which had so narrowly escaped us in 1958-59. My last season of college ball with the Mountaineers figured to be a good one, too, in which we just might take it all.

We still lacked a big man. Although he was only 6-4, Akers was moved into the pivot by Schaus, who figured it was better to have a good, tough small man there than a poor big man, which is probably true.

After I broke my nose, Mom and Dad treated me like a wounded hero home from the wars. CHARLESTON DAILY MAIL

We had another quick, gutsy, good club. Ritchie teamed with me at forward and Patrone moved up to team with Warren at guard. Posch, Goode, Paul Miller, Paul Popovich, and Ken Ward worked off the bench.

As it was, we had some kind of shooting team that season, the best the school ever had. We shot better than 46 percent from the field and better than 71 percent from the free throw line, averaged just under 90 points a game, and hit 100 or more points seven times, to tie the record we had set in my sophomore season. Personally, I hit better than 50 percent from the field again and averaged more than 28 a game. I also averaged four assists and 16 rebounds a game. And I was unanimous All-American again. We were so aggressive, we averaged more than 22 personal fouls a game, which was the second highest total in the country. Posch fouled out of seven games. Akers and Ritchie fouled out of six each. I fouled out of three. But we had to let it all out to make up for our lack of size. We were vulnerable off the boards.

We opened the season with six straight wins. Then we returned to Lexington for the Kentucky Invitational. In the first game we squeaked by St. Louis, 87-86. After Kentucky upset a powerful North Carolina team, more than 12,000 turned out to see the home side tackle us for the title.

It was a rough one. I caught an elbow under the basket and broke my nose. It would be broken many times after that, but never worse. It bled badly. And I want to tell you it hurt. But I kept playing, and I played well. I was very angry and very determined. I scored 33 points and got 18 rebounds. We won 79-70, beating Kentucky for the second time in three years and winning their tournament on their home court, which is something special.

I've always gotten a lot of publicity for playing as well as I did that night with a bleeding, broken nose. Maybe I'm a gutsy guy. Or maybe I just did what a lot of athletes would do and do all the time. What was I supposed to do, go to the bench and cry? If I hadn't been able to play well, I wouldn't have played well.

I went home for a few days then with my face all bandaged up, looking like a man from Mars, but treated by the home folks like a wounded hero home from the wars. My nose got better. I didn't get any prettier, but my nose got better. I speak with a sort of nasal twang. Breaking my nose a lot gives me a good excuse for it. Jane thought I looked pretty funny. Not pretty, but funny.

We were a big team nationally then and we were really in demand. We had a second Christmas holiday tournament that year, the Los Angeles Classic in the L.A. Sports Arena, where I was to spend so many years as a pro, though I did not know it then. California was in the tournament, too, and we left cold, snowy West Virginia for sunny southern California looking for revenge, determined to make up a little bit for our NCAA title defeat.

It was a disappointing tournament, although it looked pretty good at the start. We beat Stanford and UCLA, and Cal beat two clubs to set up the final. The final was no contest. We lost, 65-46, and it was one of the worst games one of my West Virginia teams ever played. It was my worst game in college, though I don't think I was totally to blame. I only shot five times and scored eight points.

There was talk then that there was dissension on our team, that Patrone and some others felt I was getting the ball too much and scoring too much. It's possible. But I've always been aware of being a high-scorer on my teams and have always been careful to take good shots, and have always had good shooting percentages. There have been times when I deliberately stopped shooting, though at these times the coaches always would remind me this was my job.

Honestly, if there was any bad feeling toward me I didn't know about it. I asked Schaus about it and he said he didn't think so. We had won the big tournament in Kentucky and the first two games of this tournament and the first ten games of the season. We were ranked second nationally and the only time that season we played badly was that game, so we had to have pretty good harmony and I think this was just one of those things.

We took a bad beating and I was really let down by it. Some of the guys went to the Rose Bowl game and some went to Disneyland and on the town a bit, but everyone felt bad. I just stayed in my room. I was exhausted. I think we were a very tired team just then. It happens sometimes. You get too many big, tough games in a short period and you wear thin. Maybe that was our main trouble.

We won our next six games. A couple of them tested us severely but we played well as a team and we got through them. We played at Penn State and barely won by two points, 75-73, over a team we had beaten by 30 at home. We played Villanova at home and they were 10-0 and red hot, but we took them, 89-81. They had one player, George Raveling, who was the first Negro ever to play on our home court at Morgantown. A lot has since been made of the fact that I shook his hand and put my arm around him on court before the game. I don't think I would have even done it if I had known people would make a big thing of it and I would be regarded as some sort of saint for it. I did it because he seemed like a nice guy to me and I figured he was nervous. It was just that simple.

I'm no crusader and I'm not interested in politics of any sort. I regard people only as people, and basketball players only as basketball players. I either like them or I don't. I either respect them or I don't. I don't try to make a big thing of it either way. I don't think I'm a fit judge of everyone I meet. Times have changed and there has been a lot of integration since that night in 1960, and there have been a lot of Negroes who played at Morgantown, and some who even played for Southern Conference schools, and if a white player befriends a black player today no one thinks anything of it, so let's not make too much of what I did one time a long time ago.

We went into Norfolk, Virginia, and played William & Mary at the Norfolk Arena and got beaten, 94-86. It was some kind of shock, I'll tell you. We had beaten them by 18 points at Morgantown. But then we never lost at Morgantown. And this was not at Morgantown. And they had a good team, built around a burly guy named Jeff Cohen, who was 6-6, weighed 225, threw his weight around, and could really throw up hook shots. They had us by nine at halftime and hung on. Cohen got 34. I got 42, which was my high for the season, but I fouled out with more than five minutes left, and maybe if I hadn't I could have helped us pull it out.

This was our first defeat in the Southern Conference since 1957, the first I'd ever taken part in, and ended our school's conference winning streak at 56 straight games. As I've said before, if you take an opponent lightly or if you don't play well, you can lose. That's why underdogs show up for games.

We came back to drub VMI, 101-71, and then we beat NYU, 98-69. It was considered one of the biggest wins a Mountaineer team ever scored at home, beating a good New York team the way we did. I got 35 and held Al Barden, a good player, to 11. Tom Sanders got 29, but Ritchie gave him all he could handle on the boards.

However some of the satisfaction was taken out of that right away when we flew into New York to take on St. John's in the Garden and got beaten, 79-73, in our next game. Tony Jackson and Leroy Ellis, later one of my Laker teammates, shot well for them. We went seven minutes in the second half without scoring, which cost us the game. There was a crowd of almost 15,000 there, but we didn't knock anyone's eyes out.

We had only three games left in the regular season then. We put Richmond away, 103-57. But then we took our second Southern Conference loss, 97-93, at George Washington. They had a little sophomore named Jon Feldman, who was only 5-9, but who shot holes in the basket that night with 42 points. I got 40 points and a new school record of 31 rebounds. I also got an elbow in the face and another broken nose.

It was the third time I scored 40 or more points in a game that season and two of them came in games we lost. Which maybe proves I do my best in the toughest games. Or maybe proves that this is a team game and no matter what one man does, teams win games. And lose them.

Anyway, we went home and beat Pitt easily to wind up the regular season with a fine 21-4 record, ranked sixth nationally. That was my last game on my home court in college and the school's 43rd straight home-court triumph in a

streak that was to endure only one more game the following season before it ended. I never played in a losing game
on my home court in college, and when I left the game the
fans gave me a standing ovation. It is a cliché to say it was a
thrill, but what can you say? How many people are ap-
plauded in all their lives? It's a feeling that's very difficult
to describe. I don't have all that high an opinion of myself,
but I know I'm a good basketball player, I know I always
gave it everything I had, and I was pretty proud then, as I
have been a few times in similar situations since.

We had to win our tournament to win our fifth straight
conference title and my third straight, but we weren't favored.
The team which was seeded first ahead of us, Virginia Tech,
was a good team we hadn't played during the season.

We had trouble in our opener, but wound up winning
over VMI, 90-83. I was ice cold in the first half, missing
13 of 16 shots. But Schaus said to keep shooting, so I did
and it came back and I wound up with 29. If you have a
hot man, you feed him. If not, you feed your best and hope
he comes around. I had my touch back the next night and
pumped in 36 as we trimmed William & Mary, 117-83, aveng-
ing that streak-ending setback.

The broken nose I got late in the season hadn't healed
fast. I tried a nose guard, but it was uncomfortable and affected my vision and distracted me, so I discarded it. It wasn't
anything heroic. I'm a basketball player and I can't use
something which protects me if it restricts me. One of the
William & Mary players, Bev Vaughan, also played that game
with a broken nose.

We beat Virginia Tech in the final, 82-72. It was tougher
than it seems. I didn't shoot well, scored only 14 points, and
fouled out with more than 12 minutes left to play and us
ahead by only one point. The rest of the guys, led by Warren and Petrone, picked it up and went on to win without me.
Still, I was voted the Most Valuable Player in the tournament, as I had also been the two previous years. I was later

voted team MVP and Player of the Year and Athlete of the Year in the conference for the second straight year and Schaus was voted Coach of the Year in the conference for the third straight time.

So we had another shot at the NCAA. We opened up in another triple-header in New York's Garden before more than 15,000 fans. Navy, with one of its best teams, was our opponent. They started strong, but we won, 94-86.

This took us to Charlotte for the regionals. NYU was our first foe. We had beaten them badly on our home court. Now we weren't home, but we had them on a neutral court in the South. They were a tough team, but we figured we could beat them again. But it was tough all the way.

We led by two, but they had the ball at game's end. Russ Cunningham went up to shoot and I went up with him and blocked it. But it came down in his hands and he went up again and got it off and it went in to tie it with five seconds left.

Late in overtime, I drove in for a layup that put us in front by two. Ray Paprocky hit for NYU to tie it. We lost the ball. Jim Reiss got it. Remember Jim Reiss, my teammate on the West Virginia freshman team, who transferred to NYU? He had sat on the bench almost the whole game and hadn't scored a point. He jumped, shot and scored two. We brought the ball back and I shot and missed. In the scramble, Patrone fouled Cunningham. He hit a free throw and they upped their lead to three.

We scrambled the last seconds. I grabbed a rebound and passed off to Patrone, who put it in to cut NYU's lead back to one. We scrambled some more and got the ball. In the last seconds, Schaus called for a ring of players around me, protecting me from defense. The ball was lobbed high to me. I grabbed it, spun and shot. The ball hit the iron and bounced off as the buzzer sounded. You don't always hit the big basket. I'd scored 34, but we'd needed 36. I was voted MVP of the regional for the second straight season, but we had lost the game, 82-81.

So it was all over. Almost. We still had to play the consolation game the next night against St. Joseph's of Philadelphia, which had lost to Duke. Who wanted it? Why play a consolation game? Why drag disappointed kids back for nothing? To give the fans a double-header, their money's worth, I guess. But who cares about anything but the championship game? But it was there and we had to play it, so we wanted to play it as well as we could. So did St. Joseph's. We both wanted to go out with our heads held high. We played it that way, though it was loose.

They led by eight at halftime, and still led late in the game, but we caught up and went ahead near the end and won it, 106-100. Then all we could do was put on our civvies and sit in the stands and watch NYU beat Duke in the game that counted.

So that was it, the last game of my college career. We finished 26-5. I'd played in only a dozen losses out of 93 varsity games in college, and none of them at home, so I was luckier than most. If we had not been a strong contender for national honors each of my three seasons with the Mountaineers, it wouldn't have hurt so much, maybe, but there wasn't a year I played there that we might not have won it all—but we didn't, not once, and it hurt.

I got 37 points in that last game, which gave me a new school one-season record of 908. For my three-season career, I wound up with new school records of 2,309 points and a 24.8 average. They score more now. Every year in college ball, they shoot better and score more.

If it wasn't for this book, I wouldn't speak of statistics. I never have. I can look these things up in the old record books whenever I want, and I can look at the old scrapbooks, but I never did until now, when I had to for this book. When something's done, it's done. I'm not through playing yet. Maybe when I am, when I'm old, these things will mean more to me. I think they will.

Suddenly it was over and it was sad. I walked off the court and into the dressing room and I peeled off my sweaty blue and gold uniform for the last time and I sat on a stool and I felt like crying. Then I got up and went around smiling, shaking hands with Schaus and the boys and saying goodbye, even though I'd still be seeing them in school for some time to come. We smiled and kidded around and acted like it wasn't anything so much, but we all knew it was.

For me, the season wasn't over. For me, it never seems to be. Will it some day? That's what'll be sad.

There was the Olympics. I wanted that real bad. First, I played in some post-season tournaments and special games. I played in the East-West College All-Star game in New York's Garden. Len Wilkens, who went from Providence to the pros with the Hawks, and I were elected co-captains of the East and we led a 67-66 win over the West, co-captained by Oscar Robertson and Darrall Imhoff. Then I tried out for the Olympics team at Denver.

I played on an NCAA All-Star team, along with Robertson and others. I almost didn't make it. In my first game, I missed my first twelve shots and wound up with only four points. I mean it didn't matter how good I was, how could I be picked after playing that bad? But my team won, beating the Phillip's Oilers of Bartlesville, Oklahoma, a strong AAU team. Then in our second game, I got 22 as we beat the Akron Goodyears, another AAU team. And in the championship game I got 39 as we beat the AAU champion Peoria Caterpillars, 124-97. I was taken out with four minutes to play and the fans gave me a standing ovation. Unbelievable.

I was named to the U.S. Olympic team along with six other college players—Robertson of Cincinnati, Imhoff of California, Walt Bellamy of Indiana, Terry Dischinger of Purdue, Jerry Lucas of Ohio State, and Jay Arnette of Texas. What a club that was! How would you like to have that as a pro team right now? Also on the team was Adrian Smith from the Armed Forces and Burdie Halderson, Allen Kelley, Bob Boozer and Les Lane from the AAU. It is considered the finest Olympic basketball team of all time, and I'm sure it was. And players like John Havlicek, Larry Siegfried, Don

Ohl, Tom Sanders, and Tom Meschery didn't even make it. There'd be a pretty good pro team and they didn't even make it!

So I went to Rome. The Olympics are spectacular, though we didn't have much time to watch other sports. It's fascinating meeting and making friends with people from all over the world, though. And it's interesting playing basketball against them. I wish it had been more challenging. Maybe some day soon it will be. Basketball is growing in popularity all over the world and other countries are playing it better all the time. Then we didn't lose a game. No U.S. Olympic basketball team ever has.

We scored 125 points against Japan and 107 points against Hungary. We had an interesting game against Italy and a harder game against Brazil, which was the best-schooled team we met, through they didn't come close to beating us as they had my Pan-American Games team. Our hardest game was against Russia, which was bigger and had more manpower than Brazil, but it wasn't that hard. We won, 81-57, and I scored 19 to lead all scorers.

It was a great thrill playing for my country and alongside fellows like Oscar, who is the greatest all-around basketball player I ever saw, which I will go into later. When I got up there on that victory stand to accept the gold medal for the United States, it was a thrill I'll never forget. It was something you read about as a kid and always hoped you could do. Maybe patriotism is unpopular these days, but when you're standing up there and they're playing your country's national anthem, it has to get to you.

I can't understand why so many good college and amateur basketball players turned down an opportunity to play in the Olympics in 1968 in Mexico City. Of all the excuses I've read for players not participating, the one about being too tired after a strenuous season is the thinnest.

I don't know about those who said they couldn't afford to miss their studies. I do know there was a very real problem in the Games being played so late in the year, in

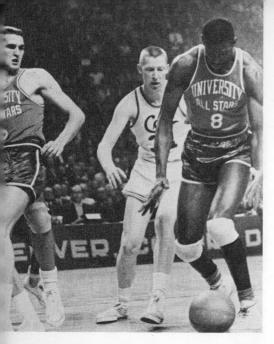

Trying out for the Olympic team with the NCAA All-Stars, I missed my first 12 shots. UPI

Our gang of future pros with Coach Pete Newell: from left to right, Darrall Imhoff, Jerry Lucas, Oscar Robertson, me, Bob Boozer and Adrian Smith. UPI

That's me grabbing a rebound against Italy at the Olympics in Rome. UPI

Oscar Robertson and I share the victory stand to accept our gold medals. UPI

October, when the pro teams already were through their pre-
season camp and exhibition games and into the regular season. For the franchise holders, it's a matter of dollars and
cents. The coaches want their players. Maybe they couldn't
get much use out of rookies who reported late. For some,
it might even cost the rookies pro jobs. Pro basketball is
the most selective of the major team sports. There are more
boys playing high school and college basketball in this country than any other sport, but there are only around 140
openings in the NBA.

I suppose, looking at it realistically, some Negroes re-
jected the opportunity as part of the protest movement by
the black community. I would not want to argue with what
anyone feels he should do to help his people, even if I do
not agree with his methods. But I've got to be honest and
say these players missed a tremendous opportunity, something very much worthwhile. There are not many ways in
which a person can represent his country and I find it hard,
myself, to understand those who don't want to.

I did, and it is one of my treasured memories.

I returned home to a hero's welcome. Even before I had left,
East Bank had a "day" in my honor. They renamed the town
"West Bank" for the day and put up signs to that effect. Bands
played and people cheered and local officials made speeches.
Two of my old coaches, Duke Shaver and Roy Williams,
spoke. I spoke, too—short and sweet. I thanked everyone. I
was really touched. I was proud before my parents, who
were there. Hometown boy makes good. How many do? After
I came back from the Olympics, there were many ceremonies, dinners, awards. It was all very nice.

I remember I received an invitation to visit the governor
of West Virginia. I presented myself to the receptionist, saying, "I'm Jerry West. I have an appointment with the Governor." And the receptionist said, "You don't have to tell
me who you are. You're better known than the Governor."

I had married Jane in Morgantown in a simple ceremony and we began a new life together, a brand new life for me, still in basketball, but on the highest, toughest level. I had left home; I had turned a corner.

The Syracuse Nats' Dave Gambee (20) and Johnny Kerr (10) watch me lay one up.

6
The Rookie

Most people can live and work where they wish. The professional athlete can't. He's at the mercy of the draft and, later on, of trades. Few athletes get to play in their home towns. Few athletes get to play where they want. Few Negroes would want to play on southern teams, for example. Sometimes an athlete can demand to be traded, and sometimes he gets his wish, but he still can't pick his spot. Depending on his sport's rules, he may be able to play out his option and try to make a deal for himself where he wants, but it doesn't usually work out too well. Clubs can't afford to let players pick their places. Everyone would go to one or two rich clubs in big cities.

Given their choice, few athletes would want to play in the smaller towns in their league. Their chances of getting a big name or a lot of money are just not as good in Detroit or Cincinnati, say, as they would be in New York or Los Angeles. Given their choice, most athletes would want to play in New York. Not that they all love New York, but they mostly all love good publicity, good salaries, and a good chance at the side money that is better in the big town than anywhere else. Everyone wants to play on a winner anywhere, but most athletes would rather play in New York than almost any other place.

As my college career neared an end, I hoped to be drafted by New York. Some people from the Knick organization had spoken to me and I knew they were interested in me. They had one of the weaker teams in the NBA, so they would have a high draft choice and might have a shot at me. All I could do was wait nervously, hoping for the best, another slave helpless before the system.

As it turned out, the league finish gave Cincinnati, Minneapolis, and New York the first selections, in that order. At that time, the league still permitted territorial draft choices. In a device to build up box office returns, the clubs had first pick on graduating collegians who had played in their territorial area. With this, Cincy figured to take Oscar Robertson, which it did.

Minneapolis needed a big center, so I kind of hoped they'd take Darrall Imhoff, leaving me for New York. But the Lakers took me, and Imhoff went to New York. I was real disappointed. I don't mean that as a knock on Minneapolis. I knew nothing about the city, except that it got real cold there. But it wasn't New York.

The Lakers had a great history back to the days when they wrapped up one NBA title after another with George Mikan, Jim Pollard, and Vern Mikkelson, but they had slipped a lot. They had a new star in Elgin Baylor, who had just completed his second season with them. They had Rod Hundley, my predecessor at West Virginia. I felt I could help them build up. But I had to talk myself into enthusiasm.

When I went to Rome for the Olympics I read in the service newspaper "Stars and Stripes" that the Minneapolis franchise was being transferred to Los Angeles. Then I got a letter from Jane telling me about it. You better believe I was excited. If New York was best, L.A. figured to be second best.

It had never been real hot basketball country and I figured it might be a while before we built up the game there, but I didn't worry about that much because I was so used to everyone being excited about the game wherever I'd played up to then. I knew the climate was great and the people lived a relaxed sort of life, which would be fine for a couple of young married kids who wanted to start a family. And it was a big town and an exciting town. Fred Schaus had left the West Virginia job to take the Laker job, which made it all the better. I knew Fred's coaching. I figured I had an in.

The Lakers offered me 15,000 dollars after some dickering and I took it. Hotshot All-Americans start a lot higher these days, but the story was different then. And they were a troubled franchise without much money to spare. Bob Short, a Minneapolis trucking man, owned the club and when he sent the general manager Lou Mohs out to L.A. to get things rolling, he told him to do the best he could with what he had. Under no circumstances was Mohs to write back for more money. So Mohs, operating on a shoestring, drummed up an office, worked out the schedule, and started selling season tickets. He got games booked in all sorts of arenas around L.A., like the Pan-Pacific Auditorium, which was a small place, and some of the small-college gyms, as well as the big Sports Arena. I couldn't hold them up. I figured if I did well and we did well, the money would pick up. Anyway, 15,000 dollars was a lot of money to me in those days. It's still a lot of money for most people, who are not lucky enough to be top pro athletes.

The NBA was a struggling organization then. It had eight teams. The East had the Boston Celtics, Philadelphia Warriors, Syracuse Nats, and New York Knicks. The Western Division had the St. Louis Hawks, Detroit Pistons, Cincinnati Royals, and the Lakers, now of Los Angeles. Boston and St. Louis, had won the divisional titles in the 1959-60 season and Boston had won its second straight playoff championship.

Boston was coached by Red Auerbach and had Bill Russell, Bob Cousy, Bill Sharman, Tom Heinsohn, Sam Jones, and K. C. Jones. Cousy and Sharman were aging veterans, but Russell had just completed his fourth season and most of the club figured to be good for a long time to come. Philadelphia had had Wilt Chamberlain for two seasons, and also had Paul Arizin and Guy Rodgers. Just as Russell had established himself as the top defensive man in the league, Wilt had established himself as the top offensive man and their duels were classics. Syracuse had Dolph Schayes and Johnny Kerr and New York had Willie Naulls and Kenney Sears as stars.

In our division, St. Louis had a physically strong club led by the great Bob Pettit, Cliff Hagan, and Clyde Lovellette. They had finished 16 games ahead of their nearest rival in the West, so it didn't figure to be easy to catch them. Detroit's best men were Gene Shue, Bailey Howell, and Walter Dukes. Cincinnati had Jack Twyman, Wayne Embry, and Bob Boozer, and now they had Oscar, too. Oscar and I were the most touted rookies coming into the league and there was a lot of talk as to which would do best. Most people figured Oscar would. He was bigger and stronger than I was and generally rated a little ahead of me. But we both had to be converted from forward to guard. Neither of us was considered tall enough to play up front in pro ball.

The Lakers' regular lineup then had Elgin Baylor and Rudy LaRusso at forwards, my old friend Rod Hundley, Bob Leonard, and Frank Selvy dividing the guard duty, and Jim Krebs and Ray Felix doing center duty. Tom Hawkins was a key reserve up front.

The Lakers were all right up front. Baylor was just brilliant. At 6-5 he wasn't a giant, but he was bull-strong and quick and very daring, the most spectacular shooter the game had ever known. He'd averaged just under 30 points a game and had taken down a lot of rebounds the season before. Big, strong, and unselfish, Rudy LaRusso went along with Elg real well.

The Laker problems were in the pivot and at the backcourt.

Felix was 6-11 and Krebs was 6-9 and both wanted to be outstanding, but neither could quite handle the great centers, though Krebs was a good shooter at times.

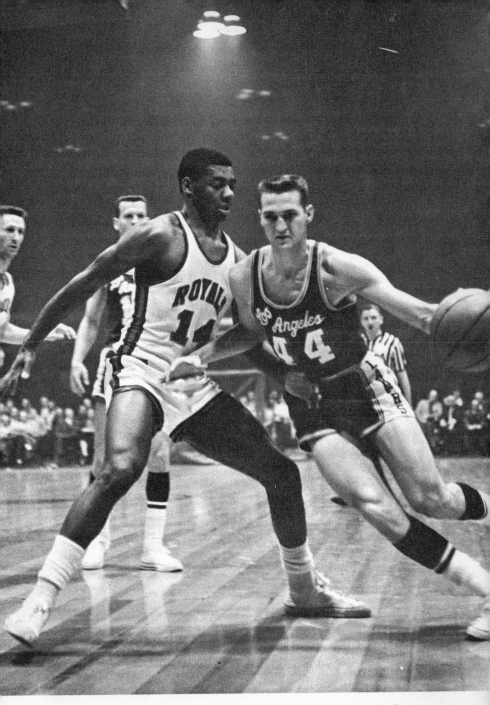

Oscar and I were the most touted rookies to come into the league.
MALCOLM W. EMMONS

Hundley, living high and not very serious about basketball, was flashy, but erratic, and wasn't scoring like he had at West Virginia. As a pro, he hadn't lived up to his college reputation. Nor had Leonard from Indiana or Selvy from Furman, both of whom had been great college players, too. Like Hundley, Leonard just wasn't serious enough about basketball. Selvy was serious, but he just couldn't get off the shots against pro defenses that he'd been able to when he led everyone in scoring in his college days.

Frankly, I expected to be a starter right off the bat and I was disappointed when I wasn't. I should have been a starter. I was better than any of our other guards. I knew it and Fred should have known it. But he'd played pro and he looked on it as a tough game and figured it would be better for me in the long run if I broke in gradually. Maybe he was right. But I don't think so. You learn more playing than sitting. And the team wasn't so good that it couldn't afford to let me play and learn. Actually, they needed what I could give them. But if I figured I had an in with Fred, I was wrong. The writers and fans got on him for not using me more, which no one would have expected, but Fred was doing what he figured was best and he stuck to his guns.

As it has turned out, I'm one of the few players in the NBA who didn't start as a regular and went on to any real stardom. Baylor, Chamberlain, Russell all started right off the bat. Oscar did, too. As a rookie that year, he left me far behind. He played all the time and averaged 30 points a game. I played part-time and averaged 17 points.

It was the worst year of my life in basketball, much worse than my first season of varsity ball in college. For one thing, of course, it was a lot harder to do well. I had to learn a new position and I had to do it playing against the greatest players in the world. In college ball, I seldom met a man who was even good enough to make the pros. Here, almost every man had been outstanding in college. And most were a lot more experienced than I was. They were used to playing night after night, traveling day after day. They were used to the life of the basketball pro. I wasn't.

As a rookie, I was treated well. My reputation preceded me, so the players probably figured they were getting someone who could help them. Thus I was accepted more readily than a player who is not well known and must show that he has something. Of course, I still had to prove myself. But a pro basketball team is a small family. Even in training camp there aren't 20 men. And it's much harder to leave a man out of things than, say, on a pro football team.

In a pro football camp, there are 35 or 40 regulars and maybe five or ten rookies who have a chance to make the team out of 20 or 30 who try out. The rookies are isolated. The regulars haze them. They have the rookies standing on the dining room tables singing their college songs. There's none of that in the NBA.

The rookies get ribbed a lot. Old Zeke, the hillbilly from Cabin Creek with the crooked nose and the nasal twang, got kidded a lot. But I still do, as far as that goes. Once I showed I could take it in good humor and wasn't all blown up about myself, it was fine.

The rookies have to do all the extra chores like help the trainer carry the gear around on trips. I did my share. Fortunately, I was no longer a rookie by the time Baylor got knee trouble. Baylor had to have all sorts of special equipment to keep his knees in shape and the rookies got bow-legged lugging this stuff around.

One thing rookies have to do now is pay the cab fares. Of course they get it back in expenses, but they've got to have it with them. We used to say the last man out would pay, but we were scrambling and crashing so hard not to be the last man out that we were sprawling all over the sidewalks, and Schaus, afraid we would get hurt, settled it by saying the last man to join up pays.

The main job of any rookie is making the club.

The first half of the season I sat on the bench a lot and suffered, watching guys play who couldn't play as well as I could. My pride was hurt. I got to play a lot, but when I got in, I was trying so hard to impress Fred and everyone that I wasn't loose and didn't make the adjustments I had to make as fast as I ordinarily might have made them.

There were times when I never thought I'd make it as a pro. I was quite discouraged until I was selected for the All-Star game. That was played in Syracuse and my West team beat the East, 153-131. I've never been able to get up high for all-star games, though it is a thrill playing on one court with all the greatest players in the game. I didn't do anything special that night, and Oscar won MVP honors. But just being picked as a rookie gave me a lift, showed me others thought highly of me, and helped rebuild my confidence.

The second half of the season, I began to play more and to start some and I began to feel better about things, and that I could make it big in the pro game. I still had bad games, but I began to have some good ones too.

One I remember came on a night when I had a bad cold. Leaving our apartment, I told Jane I probably wouldn't play. When I got to the Sports Arena, I found out Elgin was out with the flu, so I didn't tell anyone about my cold. I played the entire 48 minutes. I scored 38 points, got 15 rebounds, and we won, 126-116. It was one of only two times we beat Philly and Wilt that season.

I had another big game against Cincinnati in our final game of the season. Baylor got 49, Oscar 38, and I got 22. But in the final seconds when we were down by one, I stole the ball, passed to Baylor, took a return pass, drove around Oscar, and pumped in the shot that won it, 123-122. It was a good way to end my first season.

Our team had improved some, but we still finished seven games under .500, second in the West, but 15 games behind

A rookie has to play defense too, and I knock away a lay-up attempt in a first-round playoff game against Detroit. UPI

St. Louis. We barely nosed out Detroit, while Cincy, even with
Oscar, finished last and missed the playoffs. Boston won the
East easily, by 11 games over Philly. Syracuse placed third
and New York last.

In the playoffs we faced Detroit in our first series and beat
them, four games to two. In the deciding game, played at
Shrine Auditorium, which usually is used for operas and
things like that, and I don't think has been used for sports
since, we won, 137-120. Baylor got 35 and I got 25. I also
got a tooth knocked out, adding further to my natural beauty.

The attendance was 3,705. Pro basketball had not yet
caught on in L.A. A few years later, it would be hard to get
a seat for such a game.

We opened the Western finals in St. Louis, in Kiel Auditorium. Baylor got 44 and we upset them, 122-118. In the second game, Lovellette, Pettit, Hagan, and Larry Foust, who
were almost as big as the Los Angeles Rams' front four, overpowered us, 121-106, despite 25 by Elg. The fans got on Krebs
and waved handkerchiefs at him as he left the court after
fouling out. He complained, "They treat us like animals in a
zoo." They do, sometimes, too, though they've almost always
been kind to me, even on the road.

I think the fans in St. Louis were the toughest in the league.
At Kiel, which is a smaller building than most that have been
in the NBA, they were closer to the court than in most arenas, and it was hard not to hear them. A lot of the things
fans say are funny, though I can't think of any offhand.
Some things are nasty. In L.A. a fan with a bull-horn used
to sit right behind the visitor's bench in the Sports Arena and
second-guess the coach. I could never understand how the
coaches could concentrate, and I think such excesses should
be outlawed.

The fans are tough in Boston and Philadelphia, both places
which have been hot for basketball a long time. They root
for the home side and bear down on the officials and visiting
players very hard. If things go against them, they're ready
to fight, and sometimes the cops and special police have to

be called in. In some arenas, you have to walk through the fans to get to the dressing room and sometimes it's like walking the plank.

Basically, I have no complaint with most fans. They pay their way in and they have a right to express themselves within reason. The more excitable they are, the more rabid they are. I think the sort of support they give teams in St. Louis, Boston, and Philadelphia really helped those teams. We are only beginning to get the sort of enthusiasm for basketball that provides us this sort of support in Los Angeles.

That season we went back to L.A. to take on the Hawks at Los Angeles State College, of all places. There were just about 5,000 fans on hand and we won, 118-102. Baylor got 25 and I got 23 and we were one up on the favored Hawks again. But St. Louis bounced back right away to tie it up in the next game, 118-117. This one was tied more than 20 times before the Hawks pulled it out. Pettit got 40 points and 18 rebounds. I had a hot night, hitting 10 of 19 from the field and scoring 33.

In St. Louis we went one up again, winning 121-112 behind Baylor's 47 points and 20 rebounds. I got 24 points. We only had to beat them at home now to win the series. We couldn't do it. A record Sports Arena crowd of more than 14,000 fans turned out, but we lost, 114-113, in overtime. I hit eight of 13 shots and scored 24 points. Elgin got 39 points and 21 rebounds, but fouled out with two minutes left in overtime, which really hurt.

So it was back to St. Louis for the deciding game. Elgin and I each played all 48 minutes. He got 39 and I got 29. We shot out in front, 13-1, but they caught up and led, 49-48, at halftime. The second half seesawed back and forth. They pulled ahead near the finish, but I popped in three jumpers to narrow it to two. With three seconds left, Baylor shot off balance, but missed and we lost, 105-103.

We had come so close to winning, we were disappointed to lose. We knew we had made a far better showing than anyone expected of us, but we were still disappointed. We

St. Louis, with the great Bob Pettit (9), beat us in the Western Division playoffs in my rookie year. LESTER NEHAMKIN

dragged off court and hung our heads in the locker room and wondered how we had let it get away. We felt that if we'd had the extra home game, the final game at home, we'd have won. Maybe. Maybe not. We could have won in the sixth game at home and didn't. St. Louis got the extra home game by having had the better record in the regular season, so they deserved it.

Bill Russell is the best single defensive man ever, but here he fouled me. UPI

7
Education of a Pro

I feel about NBA playoffs like I felt about the Southern Conference playoffs. Why play all season if you're going to throw out the results and start all over again in the playoffs? The better you do in the regular season, the more money you make and the better break you get in home games in the playoffs, and there is prestige connected to winning your divisional pennant, but it's all like nothing compared to the money and prestige to be gained in the playoffs. The playoff champion is regarded as the champion and that's all there is to it. And it's not right.

In my rookie season in the NBA we carried St. Louis to seven games and almost upset them, although they proved themselves far superior to us over the full season, leading us by 15 games. I think by the end of the season we were as good as they were, but if the games you play in October and November aren't going to count, why charge for them? I understand the whole thing is good business. Battles for playoff positions are good box-office and the playoffs themselves are the best box-office of all. But it isn't a big league operation if a fourth-place team can go on to win the championship in the playoffs.

During my years in L.A., the best teams usually have won in the playoffs, but not always. We've lost the pennant and gone on to win the divisional playoff, so I've been on the lucky side of this thing and my feelings remain the same. The worst thing about it is you find you start to pace yourself during the season just so you'll be ready for the playoffs, and I never wanted to do that. It's not fair and it's not right.

The playoffs are very exciting, for the players as well as the fans. But they're so short, they're not a true test of the teams. I don't think the NBA will ever go for it, but I'd be happy if some day they went to a single championship play-off between the two division pennant-winners—a World Series of pro basketball that the two champions would have earned during the long, hard, regular season, a World Series that would make the long, hard season really meaningful.

During my first regular season in the NBA, I wound up playing in at least part of all 79 games and finished second on the team to Baylor in total minutes played and scoring. I averaged 17 points a game. Baylor averaged almost 35, second only to Wilt Chamberlain's average of 38. Elgin scored 71 points in a game at New York to set a pro basketball record for forwards and later scored 64 in a game at Philadelphia. Watching him, I first began to realize how hot a shooter could get and what the potentials were in this game.

It's a funny thing, but my 1,389 points were identical to the point with the total with which Joe Fulks of Philadelphia had won the first scoring championship of the NBA back in 1947, some 14 years earlier. But much had changed since then.

I considered my total disappointing and so did many others, both from the standpoint of my personal potential and also from the standpoint of the scoring potential for good shooters in the league. I did a little better in the playoffs, averaging 23 a game. I am proud of the fact I always did better in the pressure of the playoffs than during the regular season.

It wasn't too hard learning to play guard. In some ways, guard is a lot easier position to play than forward. You start with the ball. Moving up court, you've got the whole court in front of you. You move toward the basket and you can see everything that develops. As a forward, which I've played a few times in the pros, you get jammed into one corner of the court, you move at the basket from the side, and you've got bigger men facing you. At center, you actually play with your back to the basket most of the time. As a guard you do this on defense, and it is a handicap.

As a guard, I had to learn to handle the ball better than I had up to that time. I had to be playmaker as well as shooter. Ballhandling was the worst part of my game. I've worked on it harder than any other part of my game, and I've slowed down my pace and improved. I've worked on my dribbling and my passing and I've gained the experience you need before you know the best time to pass and the best time not to pass and the type of passes to make.

Dribbling is mainly a matter of practice. You have to keep your body between the man guarding you and the ball, of course, and you have to dribble with enough authority so you're controlling the ball and it's not controlling you. Elgin dribbles with such authority, Chick Hearn, the Laker announcer, calls it yo-yoing, which is what it looks like—just like he has the ball on a string or on a rubber band.

It's better to dribble low than high, but when you can dribble high you do because if you have your head up you can follow the flow of the action, and you can make the moves you'll want to make quickly, without having to straighten up. It's also important to be able to dribble with either hand so you can change directions quickly and still keep good control of the ball. It may sound strange, but I really learned to dribble as a pro. Teaching at summer camps, I'd have two or three quick kids try to take the ball from me. It's a tremendous exercise.

You have to dribble to move with the ball and to drive for shots, but some players dribble too much and if you don't have a shot it's better to move the ball with passes. I think Guy Rodgers, who has bounced around this league a lot, is the best all-around ballhandler, dribbler, and passer I've

I can do things I wouldn't advise most players to try. I often let my opponent get a half-step on me when I'm on defense because I find he tends to relax when he thinks he has that edge. Then I can lunge in with my long arms to steal the ball or to break up the dribble, as I'm doing here with Tom Hawkins in practice.
WEN ROBERTS

played against. Oscar is pretty close to him. He almost never makes a bad pass or has the ball stolen from him. I'm not a fancy passer, but I get the ball to the man I want to have it, which is what counts.

I believe in quick, high, hard passes, because they're the hardest to intercept. A bounce pass is easier to kick or dive at. A soft pass is easier to pick off. Of course, you have to use the pass that'll work best in the given situation. If big Wilt is drifting in toward the basket, it's often wise to lead him with a looping pass. And against the big men guarding

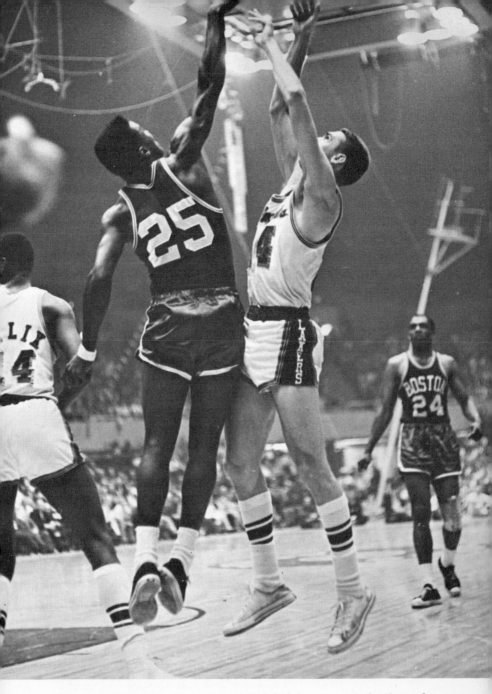

K. C. Jones was smart, strong and quick—one of the best defensive guards I've ever faced. UPI

him, it's often best for him to feed off underhand and low. The important thing is quickness. If you don't tip off your pass and you don't pass unless you have an alley to throw through, you figure to be OK. You need the alley. It's easy to see the openings from high up in the stands. It's not so easy down on the court when you are constantly screened out by a maze of fast-moving, fast-shifting, and very large men.

It's wild and confusing on the court in the middle of the action and it took a while before I got used to the moves of my teammates and my opponents and what they were apt to do in given situations, but I learned as I went along. In pro ball, unlike high school and college ball, you play against the same men over and over again, and you get a mental file on their tendencies so that you can begin to avoid doing what they're good at stopping you from doing.

Pros make up for it by being so good there's just no way you can beat them all the time. There's no way you can stop Rodgers or Robertson from making most passes. There was no way you could stop K. C. Jones from intercepting some passes. He had such an instinct for what you're going to do and he was so quick, you just couldn't beat him all the time. Jones was the best at this I ever saw. You just try to beat these men more than they beat you.

One advantage I had in my new position of guard was that I faced a lot of men who were a little smaller than the men I'd faced as a forward in college. However, the average pro is five or six inches taller and 20 to 30 pounds heavier than the average college player and they keep getting bigger all the time, so after I'd been in pro ball a few seasons, I was beginning to face guards who were 6-5 or 6-6 or 6-7 or just as big or bigger than a lot of the forwards I'd faced in college.

As a rookie in the NBA, I was 6-3 and about 175 pounds. Now, eight years later, I'm still 6-3, but I've been anywhere from 15 to 25 pounds heavier. I'm considered a small man in pro basketball today, but I think I'm stronger than I appear to be and I have unusually long arms.

Strength is very important. In pro ball they push and pull a lot. When they move, they move hard. The body contact is awful. I couldn't believe the body contact when I first got into pro ball. Basketball was designed as a no-contact game. The average pro would foul out of a college game in five minutes. But this is the pro game and anything short of murder is permitted. You have to face it and you have to live with it. You can't let them shove you around and you have to accept the bumps and bruises.

The strongest guard I've faced is Oscar. Al Attles is another real strong guy. Elgin is the strongest forward I've ever seen. He just moves men out of his way. You couldn't knock him off stride. Bob Pettit was not real strong, but he was the most agile 6-10 forward I ever faced and one of the greatest competitors. He was very determined and when he wanted to go somewhere, he went. I don't think Bob had great natural talent, as, say, Elgin does, and he wasn't smooth like Oscar or spectacular like Baylor, but he was smart and very determined. If he had a bad play or a bad game, you knew he'd come back with a good one.

The strongest center and the strongest man of all has to be Wilt. He's well above seven feet, though he doesn't let people go around measuring him, and he must weigh close to 300 pounds. He could just pick up a little guy like me and throw me into the fourth row if he wanted to, so I am grateful he doesn't want to—especially now that we're playing on the same team. The only sport in which you have to face guys as big as Wilt and Wayne Embry and Bill Bridges and Luke Jackson is pro football, and pro football players wear a ton of padding, while we go out in something like our underwear.

I try to make up for my lack of size with strength and quickness. I'm thin through the shoulders, which makes me look smaller and weaker than I am, but I have good weight for my size and I have strong arms and legs. My reach is 38 inches, which is a lot. This is more than most men who are two or three inches taller than I am, and it helps a lot. I get to balls others don't. My quickness comes naturally. I've played a lot of basketball and always paid attention to what was happening, always concentrated, and with experience I've sharpened my instinct for what men are apt to do and what is apt to happen. This helps me to put my quickness to good use.

I think the most important part of basketball is defense. I'm sure this will surprise a lot of people, but I really believe this. I think because you can practice shooting by yourself, like I did, and you can't practice stopping a shooter by yourself, most basketball players are much better shooters than defensive players. Frankly, shooters are a dime a dozen. Defensive standouts come one in a thousand. People just don't realize how important it is and players just don't work on it enough.

I always worked on my defense. Maybe it doesn't look like it, but I concentrate on it. When Bill van Breda Kolff came out of Princeton to coach the Lakers in 1967, he said I was the worst-looking defensive player he'd ever seen. I know he still thinks I do everything wrong. I do. I wouldn't teach the way I play defense, but when I do it, it works. Bill has seen this, so he's let me go my way.

There are certain fundamental rules for playing defense. First, you try to stay between your man and the basket. Second, you try to stay between your man and the man he might want to get the ball to. If a man is more of a passer than a shooter, you play him looser because you're not as concerned with him going around you. If he's more of an outside shooter than a driver, you play him tighter because you're not as concerned if he gets past you. You try to take his best shots away from him. If he goes more to his right than to his left, you play him more to his right. If he likes to shoot from just outside the free throw circle or from a corner, you try to fence him off from that area.

I lay further off my men than other defensive players. I often let them go by me, sometimes intentionally, just fooling them into thinking they've beat me. Sometimes I even lay off their strong side because I want them to go to that side, when I know they're going to do it. I sometimes get beat, but it looks like I'm getting beat a lot more than I am. The point, is I cover up. I get the man going by me, going to his strength, relaxing a little thinking he's got me beat, and then I go for him. With my quickness and my long arms, I knock the ball away or block shots. I dive for the ball a lot and get it a lot. I'm a gambler. I play unorthodox, but I do it because it's what I do best, and I get away with it because I do it well.

In my time in the NBA, the two best defensive forwards I've observed have been Woody Sauldsberry, who never got the credit he deserved, and Tom Sanders, who got credit and deserved it. They were both big and quick, they both had long arms, and they both liked to play tough defense. The two best defensive centers I've seen have been Bill Russell and Nate Thurmond. They work more at defense than Wilt does. Russell is the best, the best single defensive man ever at any position, but Thurmond is still young, very talented, and he may be on Bill's level some day.

Russell is not big for a center—only 6-10—but he's so smart and so quick he has complete control of the middle of the court. He stops guys from driving and shooting and passing near the basket because he blocks so many shots and intercepts so many passes he inhibits the other guys. You have to have the guts to play your game and the ability to play well to do a job against Bill. Frankly, I think it's the single hardest job in sports, trying to do a job against Russell.

The best guards I've ever been faced with have been K. C. Jones and Larry Costello. Jones was smart and strong and quick and he had great hands. Costello didn't have great hands, but he was strong and fast and he played his position better than anyone I've ever seen. Both of them troubled me a lot, but the offensive player has a built-in edge and there's no way you're going to beat a real good shooter consistently. The shooter knows what he's going to do, the defensive man doesn't. But if K. C. or Costello just took two or three shots away from their shooter, or stole the ball two or three times, they may have been the difference in the game. Walt Frazier of New York is an exceptional young defender, very quick, who turns a lot of games his team's way.

As a rookie in the NBA in the 1960-61 season, I had to learn how to handle great ball handlers and shot-makers, great dribblers, passers, and shooters. It wasn't easy. I didn't master the thing that season or the next season or the season after that. After nine seasons. I still haven't mastered it and after 90 seasons I wouldn't have it down pat. There is no way you can stop an Oscar Robertson or a Dave Bing all the time. Oscar has all the moves and all the shots and he does everything so effortlessly, so smoothly, you just can't anticipate him or break up his rhythm. He's the toughest man I ever tried to guard. Bing isn't in his class as a shooter, but he has so many good moves, he is so tremendously quick, and he has such desire it is hard to contain him. He has learned this pro game amazingly fast.

Actually, I'm not often assigned to the toughest offensive men. The coaches never have wanted to wear me out or foul me out. They want to save me for shooting. But in pinches I've been used on the top men and I think I have consistently done a good job on any men I faced. Playing defense is a challenge which excites me. You seldom get much credit for it, which is why many don't work on it more than they do, and it may not even be noticed if you do a bad job, but you just can't underestimate how important it is. It is more important than offense. Boston has won just about every championship in the league since I've been in it because they are the greatest defensive team, even if they're far from the greatest offensive team. Personally, I believe defense is the strongest part of my game and I'm especially proud of it.

I think being good defensively helped me make a quick adjustment to pro ball. I think more players flunk out of pro ball or fail to win the regular jobs that will give them the chance to show what they can do because they were never taught defense or never bothered to learn it, and even as pros they won't work at it hard enough to improve enough to make the grade. They think if Oscar Robertson scores 30 or 35 on them it doesn't matter. But if he scores 30 they maybe win and if he scores 35 they maybe lose, and the coach knows it.

The big shooters come out of college ball and they run into men who care about defense, so if they don't care about defense maybe they won't get to play a whole lot, and all of a sudden they're forgotten, remembered only by the alumni of their old schools from the days back when they were setting the college world on fire.

As someone who had been a big shooter in college, I found I had much to learn in pro ball. I had been able to get away with so much in college ball that I had developed some bad habits which betrayed me as a pro. I didn't drive enough, so they defended me tight. I didn't move to my left, so they defensed me to the right. I was so concerned with being a member of the team, that I passed up good shots. I was trying to be unselfish, passing off. I hadn't learned yet that when you get your shot, you've got to take it. I worried so much about other aspects of my game that I wasn't even trying to work my way into position for my good shots when I didn't have the ball.

I used to get angry at myself for every mistake I made. I'd get so angry I'd lose my concentration and play badly for a few minutes before I'd get a grip on myself again. I still get angry at myself for mistakes, but I've learned to shake them off. You don't want to forget your mistakes. You want to learn from them. But the time to think of them is between games or in practice sessions. You've got to have the concentration to put your mistakes into a corner of your mind during games and go on applying yourself to the next play and the rest of that game.

I'm just too critical of myself and too impatient with my mistakes.

It's good because I want to improve. I don't ever think I've got it made. I've seen too many players who never improve because they think they've got it made. What they do well, they enjoy doing, naturally, so that's what they practice, sort of showing off, like a great hook-shooter who spends all practice shooting hooks. I've seen too many players who won't practice what they don't do well, because they're afraid of showing these faults up, of being embarrassed by them. I always practiced ballhandling rather than shooting, because I needed ballhandling practice more than I needed shooting practice.

But being critical and impatient with myself also is bad because it upsets my concentration and depresses me. You have to think about the mistakes you've made between games, but you also have to do it in a reasonable way because you have to unwind. I brood, which keeps me wound up. I go around kicking myself in the rear end for things I did wrong or things I didn't do that I figure I should have done. No matter what I do in a game, I figure if we lost there must have been something else I could have done to help us win. I just can't stand to lose.

It's funny, but I had to learn to lose in the pro game. In high school and college, I felt bad when we lost as many as five or six games a season. In pro ball, you can easily lose that many in a week or two.

My first season as a pro, 1960-61, we lost 43 games during the regular season and six more in the playoffs. My most successful season as a pro, we lost 26 games during the regular season and again six more in the playoffs. That is a very tough adjustment to make. You never like to lose, but you have to learn that in pro ball you're going to lose so many and you're going to have to forget them and go on to the next game. You can't brood over a tough one-point loss on Saturday night, because you've got to play another game on Sunday night. You can't get down in the dumps because if you sink into a slump you can be blown right out of the race in two weeks. If you do get into a slump, you have to keep working because you play so many games that you can get right back into the race in two weeks.

Season by season, little by little, I've learned. I still take mistakes and defeats too hard, but I've learned to live with them. As a result, I'm a better player. I want to win just as much as I ever did. I try just as much as I ever did. But I'm more relaxed. Not much, but more than before.

I'd like to say I'm "up" for every game, but I'm not. No one is. I try. Most of us try. But it's just not in us. We're sick or hurting or we're tired or we've played too many games in a row or something off court is bothering us and we're just not sharp mentally and physically for every game. In high school and college ball, I'd say most players are up for every game. In pro ball, where the schedule is long, you're up for maybe two-thirds of the games. In high school and college ball you have maybe five or six big games a season. In pro ball, you can't even begin to count the games that count as big. You're no longer playing for personal satisfaction or for school spirit, for your parents or your friends or your coach; you're playing for your living.

It's a tough way to make a living. It pays off big if you're good and you're lucky. It's beautiful in many ways. But it really is a tough way to go. That first season, Jane and I found a small apartment. She was pregnant. We liked L.A. right away, but we weren't used to it and we were homesick. And I had to be away half the time.

I wasn't used to the traveling pros have to do. In college you do most of your traveling on weekends and seldom are away more than three or four days at a time. You seldom play more than two or three games a week. In pro ball, you're always traveling, you're often away for a week or two, you often play three or four games in a row. It took me a while to get used to it.

In the NBA, you're always coming from somewhere and going somewhere else. It seems like you spend most of your time driving to and from airports, sitting around airports or airplanes or hotel lobbies or hotel rooms, playing cards, watching TV, killing time. You play nights. You seldom have time to go out, even to a movie. You're always eating on the run, trying to grab a little sleep.

Playing out of L.A., we have special problems. We're three hours ahead of the East, two hours ahead of the Midwest. We get into Boston and it's time to eat there, but we're not hungry because it's not time to eat. We fly back to L.A. and when it seems to us it should be bedtime, it's time to go play a game. By bedtime we're exhausted because it was time for us to go to sleep three hours before. You live and play in a sort of a daze much of the time. It takes a long time before you get used to it and adjust to it.

We play on a lot of courts in pro ball, but in the early years of my NBA career we played on even more, like a bunch of gypsies with a roadshow putting on one-nighters in every small town we could find. We have played in Missoula, Montana, and Coos Boy, Oregon, and all sorts of places I would never have had the broadening experience to visit if I hadn't made a career of basketball.

I have no complaint with the towns, but some of the courts, even in cities that were in the league, left something to be desired. When I was a kid, I didn't think of this. In high school our dressing room was a dungeon. We played on a court with a window right behind the basket and were warned to be careful to miss the window. The first shot I took broke it.

Wilt Chamberlain is the strongest player in the game. Here I try to make one against him in a game on the old court in Charleston, West Virginia. UPI

I didn't know the old court in Charleston was as bad as it was until I went back with the Lakers and the boys pointed out a few things to me, like birds in the rafters. The old Arena in Philadelphia was the worst. It had large holes in the floor. Some places the baskets or the court were the wrong size. In Chicago, near the stockyards, they used to burn the bugs with torches before the games. The showers weren't big enough for the bugs, let alone the players. Now they play in the Stadium, which is so cold you need coats, but at least it smells better.

It's no wonder teams do worse on the road than at home. You're tired and you're playing in some strange, often sorry place. But teams are beginning to win on the road more and more because the arenas are improving. Despite the improvement, life in the NBA is still very exhausting. But we have to adjust to these conditions, because that is what we're being paid for.

8
Just One Shot

By my second season in the NBA, I had begun to adjust in every way. I knew my way around now and I knew what to expect. I was used to traveling. I couldn't sleep on planes or in the corner of coffee shops as some can, but if I got two hours to sleep in a hotel room, I could make the most of it. If my stomach told me it didn't want to eat, I didn't eat. I didn't force food down. I played hungry, if necessary. I learned to unpack as little as possible, so I could pack as fast as possible. I got used to barreling around towns, in and out of cars and cabs, in and out of hotels and airplanes, coattails flying behind me. You have to be a little crazy to do this thing. But the pay is good. And I love the game.

I got so I could put the other things aside when I got on the court, wherever it was, and play my game. Sometimes I had to look at the uniforms of the team at the other end of the court to remind myself who we were playing and where we were playing, but I got to the point where I could do a job wherever and whenever. I had learned a lot about my job as a pro guard, which is a complicated job. I had worked at ballhandling and shooting and defending, at setting up picks and using picks and getting around picks, at doing all the things you have to do, something else every second, for a 48-minute game which lasts an hour or two a night and sometimes seems to last a day or two.

The big guys aren't the only dunkers. LESTER NEHAMKIN

I watched and I worked and I learned and I became a real basketball player. I made the All-Star team at season's end, as I was to do for six straight seasons, and I finished fifth in the MVP voting. The big thing was I played. I led the Lakers in minutes played. In high school you play 32-minute games; in college you play 40-minute games; in the pros you play 48-minute games. But except for fellows like Wilt and Russell, whom coaches hate to take out even for a break, most of the regulars only play 40 minutes or so. If you're in shape, it's not too tough. By the end of a game, you're tired, but if you've played hard, you should be. If you're in shape, you bounce back by the next night.

I averaged almost 31 points a game. In my rookie season, I'd scored more than 30 in only one game. In my second season, 1961-62, I scored more than 30 in my first four games and went on from there. In December, against Detroit in Minneapolis, I got my personal career high of 47. On January 17th, against New York in Los Angeles, I upped that to 63, an NBA record for guards which still stands. I didn't even feel good that night. I had a cold going into the game. But I had a hot hand. I shot 36 times from the field and hit 22. I shot 22 times from the foul line and hit 19. The crowd was 2,766 in the Sports Arena. My big game was played virtually in private.

Exactly one week later, Cincy came to town and I got 50. In February in St. Louis, I got 45. Two nights later in a return to Morgantown we played Cincy and I showed off with 46. But it's a long game and a hot man can pile up points. One night that season, Elg got 63 in triple overtime in Philly. Later, he got 61 in a playoff in Boston. One night when Elgin wasn't playing, Rudy LaRusso got 50. Elg averaged 38. Wilt averaged 50. One night, against New York in Hershey, Pa., Wilt got 100. Against our centers, he had nights of 78, 61, 60.

One night in Detroit, I got a club record of 16 assists. Another time in Detroit, against Chicago, I got seven points in the final two minutes as we pulled one out by four. In another game against Detroit, this one in L.A., I got two free throws in the final three seconds of overtime and we won by one. I stole a ball and scored to beat Cincy by one. I sank one with seconds to play to beat St. Louis by two.

It would be easy for me to say I'm just another player on the team. I'm not. Neither is Elgin. Neither is Wilt. Neither is Russell on his team or Oscar on his. There are only five men in action on a team at any one time in basketball, and one or two men can carry a team a long way. There are single men who are of tremendous importance to their teams in other games, such as quarterbacks in football and goalies in hockey. On the day he works, a top pitcher is the most important man in a baseball game. In a given game, a slugger can hit three home runs and decide a baseball game. But game in and game out the outstanding individual is more important in basketball than in any other team game.

What Bill Russell has done for Boston, he could have done for us or several other strong teams in the NBA over the last five or six seasons. What Elgin Baylor and I did for the Lakers, we could have done for several other good clubs. What Elg could not do alone, Elg and I could do together. We need help. No one does anything alone. Johnny Unitas' passing is no good if he doesn't get time to get the ball off and if someone doesn't catch it. But Unitas doesn't need as much help as others do. Elg and I can't do anything if we don't get the ball. If we score, but the other team scores more, we haven't accomplished anything.

Elgin and I have teamed up very well. They may play this game with only one ball, but it was enough for us. We play different parts of the court and shoot from different spots. We help each other. One of us could be double-teamed. You can't put enough men on the court to afford to double-team both of us. Together, we averaged 70 points a game my second year. Together, we made the Lakers tough to beat that season and we've made them tough to beat ever since.

We had pretty much the same club we'd had the year before, but when I developed, the team developed. LaRusso, Selvy, Krebs, Hawkins, and others did their jobs. They had to be unselfish. I don't know if I could be as unselfish as guys like this. You have to have a lot inside of you to help others to the glory for the sake of the team. These guys had it. We were a happy team. We've usually had a happy team in L.A. Really. It's as big a reason for our success as any other.

It's been said that Elg and I shoot too much. Maybe this is true to the degree that the Lakers seldom get and seldom have gotten the easy baskets clubs like Boston get. But Boston had to play a team game. The Celts never had two scorers like Elg and me. Schaus always taught a freewheeling game which stressed the contributions the top individuals could make. Very often the game the Lakers have played has just been to get the ball to Elg and Jerry and let us work for our shots. But Elg and I made our shots. Would it have been smarter basketball to let others who can't shoot as well shoot more? I firmly believe I'd have scored exactly the same, even if I'd played for Boston.

Elg and I were then, and have been ever since, the leaders. It's unsaid, but accepted. We know it and everyone else on the team and everyone else in the league knows it, just as we all know Russell is Boston's leader and Oscar is Cincinnati's leader. As leaders, we have responsibilities. I know the guys count on me. In tough spots, they turn to me, or to Elg. This makes me a better player. This gives me a driving sort of determination.

One Saturday night in Boston, Ray Felix came down off the boards and landed on my right ankle, spraining it. We lost. A week later in Detroit, I drove for the basket and Baylor accidentally stepped on my right ankle, spraining it again. We lost again. We lost the next two.

We came home from a road trip and had two days off. Schaus gave us the first day to rest, but said anyone who

wanted to could practice the second day. The ankle hurt
real bad.

The next day, I figured I should turn out for the volun-
tary practice. I figured that was part of my responsibility.
The ankle was taped up. Our trainer shot it full of pain-killer.
I limped around, but said it was getting better fast.

The next night we played Philly. On one play, they tossed
a long one toward Wilt. I ran back hard, intercepted the
ball, dribbled back hard and drove in for a lay-up. I didn't
feel it during the play, but after that the ankle hurt again.

I got 36 points, 10 assists, and 10 rebounds that night.
It's a night I'm proud of. But if my ankle had been bad
enough, I couldn't have done what I did. It's that simple.
My man, Tom Gola, did get 19.

Three nights later against Syracuse, I was knocked flat and
landed heavily on my right hand and right foot. Both were
twisted and bruised. The next night, against Syracuse again,
I twisted the right ankle again.

You keep playing as long as you can play better than the
man who'll replace you and as long as you don't run a risk
of suffering a really bad injury that will sideline you for a
prolonged period. Sometimes you even take that risk.

I think pro athletes tend to play with ailments that would
put the average person in bed. It's a matter of mental con-
ditioning. You know you're supposed to, so you do it. You
never know what you can do until you try. Hockey players
get hit by pucks and badly cut, but they get stitched up and
they return to action.

I don't think I'm unique. I think I have more desire than
most athletes. Maybe that's why I'm better than an average
athlete. But many others do what I do and more.

So we slugged away the long season. Sometimes we really
slugged. Against Philly, Guy Rodgers wore me out. He was
all over me all night. He used his body and his hands so
much I lost my temper. Riled, I'm murder. I pushed him.
He pushed me. I swung and missed.

This is in the playoffs against Boston when I stole the ball from Bob Cousy and made the winning basket as the buzzer sounded.
UPI

Baylor was called into Army service at mid-season. At the time, it seemed a deathblow to our hopes. It hurt because we were having such a great season, not just another season. But I found I had something extra to give. Everyone did. We kept winning. When at season's end it was announced Elgin would have some time off for the playoffs, our hopes revived.

We wound up 54-26, the best record any of my Laker teams ever had. We beat out Cincinnati by 11 games. Detroit finished third. Aging St. Louis skidded to fourth. The new Chicago team wound up last. In the East, Boston won again, by 11 over Philly. Syracuse was third, New York fourth.

So Boston was going for a fourth consecutive NBA title. We figured if Elgin wasn't too rusty, we had a good chance to beat them. No one else did, but we did.

We had the bye, while Detroit upset Cincy to gain the Western final against us. They carried us to six games. They even led by 24 in the sixth game on their home court. But we came from behind to win it by six and settle the series. Meanwhile, Boston had an even tougher series with Philly. Russell vs. Wilt. Boston and Russell won by two in the seventh and final game in Boston.

So I had my first championship shot at Boston. I was all worked up. Too worked up. In the first game at Boston, K. C. and Cousy were all over me. I missed 17 of 22 shots and only scored 21 points. We got clobbered, 122-108. But we bounced back, and shot them down, 129-122, and evened things before heading back to L.A.

I'll never forget the next game of the series. There were more than 15,000 people in the Sports Arena. The place was a madhouse from the very beginning. It was wild all the way. We swapped with them right up to the end. But with a minute or so to play, they had us by four.

I got the ball, jumped, shot, and hit. They came down, took a shot and missed. I got the ball, jumped, shot, and hit again. Now we were tied. It was hot. The people were screaming. The noise ran right through me.

The Celtics had the ball and called time out, stopping the clock with only three seconds to play. They wanted to set up a last play. Sam Jones took the ball out for Boston. I was guarding Cousy, who was their ballhandler, and I figured they'd try to get it to him. I laid off him a little, to let them try. As Sam's hands began to move, I began to move. As the ball was thrown toward Cousy, I lunged in front of him and grabbed it. I pushed it in front of me and followed it. Dribbling, I was scared the buzzer would go off. I pulled the ball off my dribble, jumped, leaned toward the backboard and laid the ball into the basket. As it was coming through the cords, the buzzer sounded. We won, 117-115.

The place went crazy. People were jumping up and down running out on the court and screaming. My teammates were all over me, slapping at me, grinning at me, yelling at me. I don't even remember getting through that mob scene and down to the dressing room. There was bedlam all over again. It was New Year's Eve, the end of a war, and everyone's birthday all at the same time. The writers came at me. What could I tell them? They saw it. Let them write it. I got out of there finally and got my wife and took her home. We kept talking about it. I was so excited I was like a little boy.

That night I lay in bed thinking about it. I've never forgotten it. Everyone wants to hit a home run in the ninth inning to win a big game. That was my home run. I was Bobby Thomson hitting one out in the ninth inning to win the playoff for the Giants against the Dodgers. I've had far more than my share of big plays, big baskets, big moments, but that was it for me. I haven't talked about it in a long time. But if I could have bronzed that moment, I would have. It's my trophy, and if I could put it up on the mantlepiece, I would. I read about it once in a while, but people mostly have forgotten about it.

Maybe if we'd won that series from Boston, it wouldn't have been forgotten.

Maybe we were too high for the next game. Boston knocked us off, 115-103, evening the series, and we went back to

Boston. If Elg was rusty, he didn't show it. He hit 22 of 46 shots and scored 61 points, which still stands as a playoff record, and we won, 126-121, to go ahead, three games to two. We had the sixth game at home and had a good chance to wrap it up as we went back to L.A.

We got off fast and led by eight at halftime. We knew it would be tough, but we figured we had them on the run. Maybe we were overconfident. We went out and stood around at the start of the second half. I didn't work for shots and didn't shoot much. I was very tired, but I should have forced myself. Sam Jones got hot and they caught up and went past us and led by 10 after three quarters. They won by 14.

So it was back to Boston for the seventh and final game. It was some game. The lead changed hands 13 times. Baylor was cold, but he kept working. He hit 13 out of 40 shots and scored 41 points before he fouled out in overtime. I hit 14 of 30 and got 35 points. Russell got 35 points and 40 rebounds. He is some kind of a man. He was all over us the whole series, blocking shots, clearing the boards, intimidating us, controlling the action. He's not a great shooter, but in the big one he was even sinking baskets. Still, we almost overcame him, we almost beat Boston in this one.

Pops Selvy hit his second straight basket to tie things at 100-all with 18 seconds left in regulation time. Boston tried to kill the clock to set up the winning basket, but lost the ball. We brought it in to the offensive zone. Russell and the Celtics, toughest ever defensively, couldn't afford to foul, but they couldn't afford to give us too much room either. They were all over us.

Selvy got the ball in the open. He had his shot, a short one from the side. He took it with three seconds left. He missed it. What can I say? I should have had the shot? Maybe. I wanted it. I think I'd have made it. But I always think that. Selvy was hot and he had his shot and he should have taken it and he did. And if he'd made it, I'd never have thought anyone else should have had it. He didn't make it. So there we were still tied.

We huddled before overtime. I remember seeing Russell sitting on a stool near the Boston bench in the excitement of that packed dark, old Boston Garden. His body seemed limp. His head was hung. Sweat was just pouring off him. I figured he had nothing left. We had won six straight overtime games. We were good in overtime games. I figured we'd win this one.

Baylor fouled out. But so did Sanders for Boston, and their Heinsohn and Loscutoff had already fouled out. Russell didn't. Rousing himself somehow, he was magnificent. They got three points on us. At the buzzer, it was 110-107. And it was Boston's Celtics jumping around, while we slumped off. The Boston fans practically ran over us to get at their heroes.

Maybe if Baylor hadn't been in the Army . . . but he played as well as he ever did in those playoffs. Should we crucify Selvy, a fine player? If he'd had a second shot, even in the same situation, I think he'd have made it. Just one more chance. But you only get one chance at a time. You either do it or you don't. That's the way it is in sports .

When Jerry Lucas joined Cincinnati everyone thought the Royals would challenge Boston. MALCOLM W. EMMONS

9
The Long Season

We figured we were on the verge of winning everything. We were right. We were on the verge. But we stayed there. In my third season as a pro, 1962-63, I suffered the first of what was to be a series of serious injuries in my NBA career. That was one thing that held us back that season.

We had one of the best clubs we've had since I've been in Los Angeles. We added Dick Barnett, a guard, Gene Wiley, a center, and LeRoy Ellis, a center and forward.

Ellis was 6-11 but skinny and unsure of himself. He'd learn, and would help more later. Wiley was 6-11, too, and he took Felix's place, sharing center with Krebs. He had some talent, especially on defense, and he helped, but he lacked fire. We were still weak at center. But Barnett bolstered our bench. He was a tremendous shooter. He shot his jump-shot falling backward. It looked like he'd land on his tail. "Fall back, baby," Chick Hearn would shout every time Dick would shoot. Barnett was one of those guys who could come in cold and get hot. He made things happen, which is what you want in a bench man. When you go to a sub, you usually want to stir things up. Dick averaged 18 points a game. Elg, back from his short stint in the Army, averaged 34. I averaged 26, but only played 56 games. We missed Tom Hawkins, traded to Cincy for a draft pick.

The league had improved. Cincinnati added Jerry Lucas, a great high school and college player, and a very fine, if not a great pro player. Lucas does everything well, but he seems to have trouble working himself up. But with Robertson and Twyman, he gave the Royals a lot of strength. Some thought they'd give Boston trouble, but they were wrong. Boston was too good. They added John Havlicek, who made them even better. He was even better coming off the bench than Barnett. He always seemed to hit his first five shots. Frank Ramsey used to do that for Boston, and even before he retired they came up with Havlicek. On most clubs he'd have started, but the fact is he was more valuable coming off the bench. He's quick and versatile. He can play guard or forward. He never has a real good shooting percentage, but I never noticed: he always hit against us.

Our division had gotten a lot tougher because the Philadelphia club, with Chamberlain, had moved to San Francisco to set up a natural rivalry with our Los Angeles team. Things didn't go smoothly for the Warriors in San Francisco at first and they lost a lot more games than they won, even with Wilt, but they usually were tough to play, because of Wilt. He couldn't seem to decide how to play, whether to shoot more or pass off more. It was impossible to stop him from scoring a lot, but when he was shooting a lot it wasn't hard to contain the rest of the club and outscore them as a club.

St. Louis still had Bob Pettit and Len Wilkens but Clyde Lovellette was sent to Boston. However, the Hawks added Bill Bridges, a rugged rebounder, and Zelmo Beatty, a strong young center, and started on the way back. Detroit had Bailey Howell and Don Ohl and added Dave DeBusschere, a fine forward, who at the age of 24 became their very young coach. Chicago had only Walt Bellamy, the big center.

No one was easy, really, but we were too good for this division. From late in December to the middle of January, we won 11 straight games, a club record. We won and won and won and we seldom lost. I had some big games, especially on the road. I had 49 one night in San Francisco and 46 another night in St. Louis. The 22 best-scoring games of the season, right up to 73, were all Wilt's. He averaged 44. But the Warriors kept losing.

We kept winning until I got hurt. Diving for a ball against New York, I tore a hamstring muscle. The pain was just awful. I tried to get around, but couldn't. When the doctor shoved a needle in my leg a few days later, I wanted to shout. I sat half-naked on the training table, sweating and suffering and feeling sick, figuring the beautiful season was ruined.

I missed 24 games, just about the last third of the season. I limped around with my leg all bandaged up and tried to practice, but couldn't. I sat on the bench and watched us lose 15 of our last games and felt really bad. Still, we'd built a big 10-game edge and St. Louis couldn't catch us. We wound up 53-27, only one game worse than the year before and five games better than St. Louis. Detroit was third. San Francisco and Chicago blew the playoffs. In the East, Boston beat Syracuse by 10 games. Cincy was third and New York missed the playoffs again.

I was back for the playoffs, but I wasn't at my best. St. Louis quickly wiped out Detroit and came at us very determinedly. We stood firm. I remember they led us in one game by seven points with 70 seconds to play. I sank a couple and we caught up with seven seconds to go, but St. Louis had the ball for the last shot. Cliff Hagan was dribbling across midcourt. He wasn't my man. He wasn't looking for me. I didn't figure he would be. I crept in, dove, and knocked the ball away. I was so anxious to get it, I stumbled right over him. But I got it and drove. I wasn't sure how much time was left. I was afraid to go all the way in. At the free throw line I stopped, grabbed the ball, jumped, and shot. As it went through, the buzzer blew. We won, 101-99. We won the series in the seventh game, 115-100.

So we got Boston again. But they were better than they'd been the year before and we weren't as good. They didn't have a man who averaged 20 points, much less 30, but they had two men who averaged 10 each and one who averaged

Tom Sanders is the kind of guy who will defense you to death. UPI

13 and one who averaged 14 and one who averaged 16 and one who averaged 18 and one who averaged 19. They had some kind of depth and balance. They had guys like Havlicek and Ramsey and Lovellette coming off the bench and guys like Sanders and K. C. Jones who defensed you to death and guys like Heinsohn and Sam Jones who could shoot holes in the basket when they got hot. They still had Cousy, who could do more tricks with a basketball than any man I ever saw. And they had Russell, who was the big one.

The Celtics swept the first two at Boston, 117-114 and 113-106. You have to win one on the road if you have only three at home—if you're going to win the series. Usually, you have to win one or two on the road to win the series even if you have the extra game at home. It helps a lot if you can win one early. You don't give up. You don't say to yourself, "Well, that's it." You keep showing up. But you know you're in a bad hole and the odds are running against you and it puts a lot of pressure on you.

Now we just *had* to win the first one at home. In fact, we had to win the next two at home. We won the first, 119-97. We blasted them off the court. Baylor and I were both hot. He got 38 and I got 42. A record Sports Arena crowd of 15,493 went wild. There were only a few less people the next game. But we lost, 108-105. They had us down, but we closed to within four at the finish. Russell turned for a short hook and collided with Elg. The ref let it go. They won, 108-105. They deserved it. I got 18. I was rotten.

Boston went home to wrap it up, but we were stubborn. Elg got 43 and I got 32 and we surprised them, 126-119. They were so upset they argued the referees into technical fouls. So we had a chance to even it back in Los Angeles. Another record Sports Arena crowd, 15,521, turned out. Some 6,000 were turned away. They missed Bob Cousy's farewell appearance. Boston blasted us. They led by as many as 16. We tried to pull it out at the finish, but they held on, 112-109, to settle it in six. That made it five straight titles for Boston.

They played with the confidence of a team that had won a lot of championships, but they hustled like a team that was hungry for its first one. If there was a loose ball, they got it. They didn't really have a big team; they had small, quick, hustling men and they always seemed to want the ball more than anyone else wanted it. I don't know how good a coach Red Auerbach was. He was always playing the angles. I don't think he knew more basketball than anyone else. But he was a psychologist, lighting a fire under his guys, lighting up those big cigars of his every time his team had a game wrapped up. I do know his teams always hustled, which is a big thing. And I know his teams won, which is all that counts.

They were even better, the next season, 1963-64. Cousy, Ramsey, and Jim Loscutoff retired, and Willie Naulls was the only player of consequence they added, but I honestly believe this was the best team I've seen since I've been in the NBA.

Cousy was great. Unfortunately, I saw him only at the end of his career when he undoubtedly was past his peak, but I could see why he was regarded as the most spectacular little man ever to play in the NBA. He was a brilliant and flashy ballhandler and the greatest long passer I ever saw, though Oscar was and is the best short passer. Bob was also well regarded as a person, sort of the unofficial spokesman for the players in the league, so Boston undoubtedly missed his leadership. But he did not seem to me to be an outstanding defensive ball player and when Boston got K. C. Jones into the regular lineup, and off the bench where he was being wasted, the Celtics' defense became tough all over the court, their greatest asset, and their team play seemed to pick up.

They still had that great balance and plenty of depth. They seemed to mature and they were tougher to beat than ever. They had to be. Cincy came up with a great season and came within four games of the Celts. The Syracuse club was moved to Philadelphia and finished third. Dolph Schayes had retired and they missed him a great deal. New York, as usual, was last. They traded Richie Guerin and had no one left.

We had the worst season I ever had in Los Angeles. It's hard to explain. We just couldn't seem to get untracked. I averaged 28, but broke my thumb on Wilt's shinbone trying to steal a ball from him, and missed eight games, Baylor averaged 25, limping around on bad knees. Barnett averaged 18. Without him we'd have been in worse trouble than we were. LaRusso didn't have a good year. Our centers were slaughtered. Hundley retired. We added Don Nelson, who was handy, and Jim King, who was a good guard prospect, but they didn't play much.

Once again, the others in the division improved enormously. Chicago, with Walt Bellamy, moved to Baltimore and added a flashy rookie forward, Gus Johnson. The Bullets finished fourth, ahead of Detroit. St. Louis, with Guerin, who gave them a lot of aggressiveness and shooting from the backcourt, beat us out. But the divisional title went to San Francisco. They drafted Nate Thurmond, a 6-11 rookie, a fine, unselfish ball player. With Wilt at center, San Francisco used Nate in a corner and between them they dominated the backboards. Guy Rodgers played well in the backcourt. Alex Hannum did a marvelous job of getting them to pull together.

There were some good moments. We swept Boston two straight games in L.A. one weekend. We beat them in overtime, 125-118. I got 36; Barnett got 30, including 14 in the fourth quarter and seven in the overtime. That's clutch shooting. Then we beat them, 97-95. Barnett only got 14, but his two free throws won it. I had 47 in a win in New York. I couldn't find the basket and went scoreless in the first period. I couldn't miss it in the last three periods. I could have hit with watermelons from midcourt. You never know. One night I got 41 in a win over Philly in Syracuse, then two nights later I got 42 in a win over Detroit in the Sports Arena. In a game with Cincy, Oscar and I had one of those duels everyone was always looking for. In this one I got 37 and

he got 36. I scored 11 points in a little more than two minutes to settle it.

After I broke my thumb on Wilt, I figured I could play
with it splinted and taped. But it took two weeks before I
could handle the ball well enough to return to action. We
lost nine out of 10. We were 31-19 before I got hurt. We
were 11-19 afterward. We wound up only four games over
.500—four games behind St. Louis and six behind San Francisco.

I was hurting and we were dragging as we went into the
playoffs. We carried St. Louis to the limit, but lost three games
to two in a best-of-five series. Boston won the championship
over San Francisco, four games to one. It was Boston's year,
as usual.

It was the Celtics' sixth straight NBA title and fourth straight
since I had come into the league. They had the best team
all those years. There is absolutely no question of that. We
knew that. Maybe it affected our play. There were spots
where one of us might have caught them off guard, upset
them, nosed them out, but we didn't do it. We tried, but we
didn't do it. They were the best team. Absolutely no doubt
about it.

We were better than we showed that season. All the long
summer we thought about that and we were determined to
bounce back. We did. Imhoff, who had gone from New York
to Detroit, now bounced to us. We added Walt Hazzard, a
flashy guard, who'd led UCLA to the NCAA championship.
We suffered a psychological loss when Jim Krebs, who had
been planning to retire, was killed that summer in a freak
accident. We all felt awful about his death. It stayed with us
through the season.

St. Louis was still very strong, though Bob Pettit, playing
his last season, was hurt a good bit. Baltimore added Bailey
Howell and Don Ohl in a big deal with Detroit, giving up
Terry Dischinger and Rod Thorn. Detroit also added a good
shooting rookie, Eddie Miles. San Francisco made the biggest
deal, trading Chamberlain back to his home town, Philadel-

phia, for three minor players and money. Wilt may require special treatment, but without him San Francisco sank into the cellar. At one point they lost 17 straight games, an NBA record.

Boston, pretty much standing pat, was still the best in the East. Cincinnati was next best. Then came Philly, with Wilt. The 76ers added Luke Jackson, a powerful forward. They were on the verge of great things. New York was outclassed, but the Knicks made progress with the addition of Willis Reed, a big, strong center-forward.

We had a fine season and I had my best ever. I avoided serious injuries, played all 74 games, and led the team in minutes played with 3,066. I may look skinny, but I'm strong enough. If I'm not injured, I can play most of every game. We play a tough schedule, but the more I play, the sharper I get. Up to a point. If we play two or three games in a row, or in four or five days, I may feel a little tired, but I'm usually sharp and I don't mind. Sometimes in this league the schedule is too much. If I play four games in a row or five or six games in a week, I do wear down. But then, so does everyone who has to go through a period like that. I wouldn't want to wrestle with Wilt, but I keep in shape and I'm able to play as much as almost anyone in the league, as long as I'm not hurt. I broke my nose again that season, but I don't even count that. I tape it up and play. I'm used to broken noses.

I scored 40 or more points 15 times that season—seven times in the regular season and then eight times in the play-offs. My high was 53 against Cincinnati in Los Angeles late in January. I hit 21 out of 36 from the field that night, but I got two extra overtimes to run my scoring to my second highest ever. I got 47 at New York three nights earlier. I got 43 against Detroit in Pittsburgh, 44 against Philadelphia at Syracuse, and 44 against San Francisco in Los Angeles. I am just as proud, however, of a night in November against Detroit when I tied my own club record with 16 assists. I averaged 31 points a game during the season, second only to

I broke my nose again, but I just tape it up and continue to play.
DARRYL NORENBERG

Wilt Chamberlain's 34 in the NBA. Elgin averaged 27 and we put together a 49-31 record, winning the West by four games over St. Louis for our third pennant in my five seasons in the league.

The game I remember best was against Cincinnati in Los Angeles in January. In the first half I could not find the basket. I'd have been just as well off shooting blindfolded. In the second half I scored 39 points. I could have found the basket blindfolded, I'm sure. I could have bounced the ball in or kicked it in. For 24 minutes I couldn't believe myself. In the first half, they'd led us by as many as 24 points. In the second half we caught up. They still led us by two points with five seconds to play when I shot a jumper from about eight feet out and missed. I drove right on toward the backboard, took the rebound with one hand, and shoveled it through a swarm of Royals toward the basket. It swished as the buzzer sounded. We went on to win in overtime.

You never know in pro basketball. There is not another game that compares to it when it comes to turning a lopsided game around in a hurry. You score points so easily in this game, you can score so many so quickly, you can get hot and overcome a seemingly insurmountable lead in a hurry. Because of this, it's hard to quit. They say the last two minutes are all that counts in pro basketball. It may be a weakness of the game, but I think it is generally true. Of course, every point counts and you have to hustle all of the time, but most of the time it does seem that there is not a great deal of difference between the various clubs, and the breaks even out and the game is decided in those last two minutes.

If that is a weakness of the game, it is also a strength. You can never give up on a pro basketball game. One game we led by four and had the ball with 15 seconds to go and lost. You just never know.

We finished the season tremendously strong. In the playoffs Baltimore upset St. Louis and then challenged us in the Western Division playoff finals. In the first game, played in Los Angeles, Baylor went up for a twisting shot and came down

With Baylor injured, I had to try harder in the playoffs, and here
I'm trying to get one off against Baltimore's Walt Bellamy. UPI

in a pile of pain. There was a loud "pop," which you could hear all over the court. He got up and tried to run after the play, but collapsed again. He had to be helped off the court.

Elg had been building up calcium deposits in his knees which were like small grains of salt rubbing painfully inside his knees. However, the doctor had decided that it would cause more damage to operate than to try to toughen the joint with exercise, and Elg had been playing in considerable discomfort. Late in the season, he fell on a court in Cleveland which had been laid on a hard concrete floor. Possibly he cracked his right kneecap then.

In any event, in the first playoff game of our Baltimore series, part of his kneecap tore away. He had to be taken to the hospital for an operation. He was out for the series. Everybody thought he would be lucky to ever play again.

We stood in a huddle with Schaus. What does a coach say to a team at a time like this? "We'll all have to try harder," he said. What else can you say? You *can* try harder. And sometimes you can do far more than you think you can. Our high hopes had been broken along with Baylor's kneecap, but we had to give it everything we had left. I knew the guys would be looking to me now, counting on me. I was very determined. I began to play with all I had in me. I worked and worked and worked and when I felt too tired to take even one more step, I pushed myself further. When Dick Barnett, our next best shooter, pulled a groin muscle in that series, and was severely handicapped the rest of the way, I pushed myself further yet. Everyone pushed himself as far as he could go. I was the scoring leader, but everyone—Darrall, Rudy, LeRoy, Jim King—did everything he could.

I scored 49 points in the first game and we beat the Bullets, 121-115. Two nights later I scored 52 and we beat them again, 118-115. It was an NBA playoff record for guards. We were behind by one point with 20 seconds to play when Ellis, who's 6-10, went up with Bellamy, who's 6-11, for a rebound. They both got their hands on the ball. I had sneaked in between them, leaped, stole it, and dropped in a basket to put us in front by one. They still had time for another shot. They brought the ball down. On a pass, I lunged, intercepted the ball and drove for the basket. I was fouled and sank two free throws to wrap it up at the buzzer.

Two nights later, in Baltimore, I scored 44, but we lost to the Bullets, 122-115. In the next game I scored 48, but we lost to them again, 114-112. I almost had 50. I had it when I hit a jumper to put us ahead in the final seconds, but it was taken away when referee Joe Gushue whistled a foul on LaRusso for an illegal screen, nullifying the basket. Baltimore got the ball and Don Ohl banged in the winning bucket. That one really hurt. But two nights later, back home, I scored 43 and we beat them, 120-112. And two nights after that, back in Baltimore for the sixth game, I scored 42 and we wrapped up the series, 117-115.

In six games over 11 days, I scored 277 points and we had won a series we had no business winning. There were many times in my career when I scored big or played well, yet this was not the main reason we won games. But I know that I was the main reason we won that series in early April of 1965. I think I responded to the challenge of leadership I faced with Elgin out. I wouldn't have done what I did had Elg been playing. I wouldn't have had to. Everyone said then and many have said since that this was the hottest streak, the greatest single series any basketball player has ever had. I'm real proud of that. In a way, I was lucky. In another way, I wasn't. Without Elg, I was roused to do this big thing I did. Without Elg, I shot more than I ordinarily would have.

I'd like to be able to say now that I single-handedly carried my team past Boston in the finals. I can't. There was no way I could have done that, even if I hadn't been exhausted. And I was exhausted. I felt absolutely drained dry and worn out. I could hardly rouse myself to move between games. When the games came, I had to make myself go out and play. It is a long season. It begins with exhibition games at the end of September and ends with playoff games seven or eight months later. In between, you travel countless thousands of miles and play maybe a hundred games. If you're not going anywhere as a team, the last month of the season is horrible. Some nights you'd as soon have pneumonia as have to go to the arena. If you're in a pennant race, it carries you along. The playoffs always give you a lift. But after our first series in the playoffs, I didn't have much left.

None of us did. Our first game in Boston, they wiped up the court with us, 142-110. It was humiliating. We've always had a gutsy club. Somehow, we pulled ourselves together to give it another go the next night. They beat us again, but only 129-123 this time. I got 45. When we resumed the series in Los Angeles, we took them apart, 126-105, as I got 43. It was just one of those games. It didn't mean anything. It was a dying gasp. Two nights later, they put it to us, 112-99. If I was responsible for some of our earlier victories, I was responsible for this loss. I had my shots, but they kept bouncing off the iron. I missed my first five or six. I lost my touch. I tried to think them in. I kept shooting. Later, people asked me why. There was no one else to shoot. I had to. Usually you don't stay cold a whole game. I did. I missed 21 out of 27 shots.

In Boston, the Celtics wrapped up another NBA title, 129-96. It wasn't even close.

Baylor shows some of his great body control.
MALCOLM W. EMMONS

10
Mr. Clutch

After that series with Boston I felt like a giant weight had been lifted from my back. I was disappointed, but when it was finally over and there wasn't anything else I could do about it, I was really relieved that it was done. Now it's just a memory, and despite the defeat, not the worst memory I've ever had. I set a playoff record that still stands with an average of more than 40 points a game. I was third to Russell and Robertson in the voting for the Most Valuable Player award in the league. I've never won it. To be honest, I think maybe I should have won it that year. Elgin never won it, either, however, and he certainly has to be on any all-time all-star team. Oscar won it once. Since I came into the league, Russell won it five times and Wilt twice.

I can't argue with this, really. The big center is more valuable to his team than any other man. He controls the game more than any other man. No one, not even Wilt, rates close to Russell as the most valuable player I've seen in this league. Wilt is bigger and more talented, but I do not think he is as dedicated or as flexible. He has been just fabulous and I would not want to demean him in any way, even if he was not on my team now; but Russell has dominated games in this league as no one else ever has and possibly ever will. Bill is not a great shooter, but he is a great rebounder and a great defensive player. He has found a way to play that works and he has been absolutely brilliant and unsparing of himself in sticking to it. His record speaks for itself. More than all of the other Celtics, he is responsible for that Boston record.

Oscar Robertson is the single most talented man I've ever observed in this game. There is not anything he does not do brilliantly. And he does everything naturally. He seems to have been born with a rhythm for basketball that no other man has ever had. Only Elgin rates close to him in this regard. Elgin can also do it all, and do it all well. Throw in Bob Pettit at forward and K. C. Jones at guard and you've got my all-star team of the men I've seen since I've been in the league.

Being a smaller man and a guard, Oscar has not been able to dominate games the way Russell has or thus be as valuable as Russell has been. But for sheer talent I consider Robertson the best I've ever faced.

Who's better, Oscar or me? This is the one single question that has been asked more often than any other since I've been playing basketball. And it is really for others to decide, if it can be decided. But I personally have always felt that Oscar was the best.

He has had two big advantages over me. Number one: while we play the same position, he has greater size, which gives him some advantages. And number two: he's a better ballhandler and passer. That's for sure. I think we're about equal as shooters. I'm a better outside shooter, but Oscar is better inside. I may have two advantages over him. One, I'm better defensively. And two (and I'm being so honest about this that it scares me a little), I do believe I've played better and done more than he has in certain situations when it counts the most.

Possibly I have had more opportunities in clutch situations than Oscar has. I think I've had more help than Oscar has had, too. I think it's very difficult to compare the contributions of two men playing on two different teams in two different divisions. And I guess we had better leave it at that.

I peaked as a shooter during the 1964-65 season. I averaged 31 points a game and set a team record for accuracy. I hit 137 free throws in the playoffs, a league record, and in one stretch I scored 31 foul shots in a row. To some extent, statistics lie. Rarely do they tell all of the story. But these do say that I'm a good shooter.

I've mentioned that when I was a rookie I seldom went to my left for shots. In the following seasons I compensated for this—not by going more to my left, but by shooting quicker. I'm not giving much away. In his first year as coach, during the 1967-68 season, Bill van Breda Kolff noticed that I never went to my left for a shot. The defensive players who can use this information know it. The others don't matter. I don't think it matters anyway. They say a good shooter has to move both ways, but really it's not true. I don't think there are many shooters in this league who go both ways. Some are more versatile than others. Some can shoot outside and drive equally well. Not many. Most of us have one or two favored spots we shoot from. The more you have, the better off you are and the worse off your defender is.

Some say you can tell how good a basketball player is by how he plays without the ball. Originally, I frequently brought the ball downcourt for the Lakers. I liked it because I felt I was in control of the play. If I wanted to move for a shot, I could. Then Schaus began to have others bring the ball down, to save me from wearing down. I had to learn to move without the ball, to get into position for shots without the ball, to set up screens for other shooters. It was a tough adjustment to make. Now, with our veteran guards gone and new men brought in since we acquired Wilt, I'm handling the ball more again.

When I do get the ball, I try not to give anything away. I protect the ball with my body, keeping my body between the ball and the defender. I try not to show by my eyes or my hands or my feet or the way I'm going at things just what

I'm going to do. The defense may figure I'm going to shoot, but they can't be sure, and they don't know what kind of shot I'll take or where I'll take it from and when.

A lot of guys think you have to make a lot of fakes. I don't. I throw only enough fakes so the defense is looking for them. Many times the best fake is no fake at all. Quickness in shooting or passing is much more important. However, there is a sort of fake I do use sometimes which is highly unorthodox. Sometimes I'll expose the ball, as when I'm dribbling. I tempt the guard to go for it. When he does, I make my move. The key thing here is that I'm deliberately tempting him and waiting for his move.

I feel more comfortable going to my right than to my left so I most often go to my right. The defense still doesn't know when and where I'll make the move to shoot. I'm a better jump shooter than a driver and every good defensive man in the league knows this and plays me tight to try and take the jumper away from me. However, because the defense plays me tight, it is vulnerable to my drive. I'm not a great dribbler and I'm not powerful enough to muscle my way in, but I drive enough to keep the defense at least fairly honest.

I'm at my best from about 15 feet away, but I have a wider range than many shooters. In practice in college, Schaus used to throw me the ball at different places and I'd shoot it wherever I got it, whenever I got it, bang, bang. I'm naturally quick and I worked to get quicker and to broaden my variety of shots. Straightaway speed means little, but quickness means a lot. I make my move quickly and I think I probably have the quickest release of the ball in the league. I still use the drill and I still work on quickness.

Some jump shooters go very high, then seem to hang in the air before they shoot. I think they overdo it. I think they get out of whack trying to go too high and hang too long. I actually shoot on the way up most of the time. It's all one connected motion. I was able to build a consistent rhythm this way. Usually, you can't jump higher than men two or three inches taller than you. Unless you're the world's greatest jumper, there's always going to be someone able to jump higher, anyway. It's the surprise of your move and the quickness of your move that's going to beat him, not the height of your jump. I imagine I have fewer shots blocked than anyone in the league.

You still have to put the ball in the basket. One of the most important things is to jump straight up. Even more important is to jump the same way every time. If you're off balance, your chances of executing a good shot are not very good. Dick Barnett shoots falling away, but at least he always shoots falling away. He feels in balance this way. He's grooved this way. I try very hard to jump straight up, no matter how hard and fast I've been moving. In practice, I pick spots on the court, move to them, jump, shoot, and try to come down in exactly the same spot as my last footsteps. When I'm doing it consistently I seem to hit consistently. By doing this I've eliminated at least my sideways mistakes.

When I'm shooting, I move the ball to my palm, cock my wrist a lot, and extend my arm straight toward the basket, rolling the ball off my fingertips. By cocking my wrist I seem to get a good follow through, winding up with my arm pointing straight over the basket. Most people tell you to cradle the ball on your fingertips, not your palm. I think it's too easy to twist your hand or wrist when you have the ball on your fingertips, and too easy to lose control of the ball. I seem to get a better feel of the ball on my palm. When I shoot, the ball will roll off my fingertips anyway. I'm guiding the ball with my whole hand, not just my fingers.

The more cocked my wrist is when I release the ball, the softer my shot, which is important because if I'm not deadly accurate a soft ball will hang on the rim and maybe roll in. And I use a medium-flat arc. But if you want to keep your defenders off balance and avoid blocks, and if you want to be able to take advantage of all of the offensive opportunities that come along, you have to be able to change up the way pitchers do in baseball. You need more than one pitch, in other words. You just have to practice until you've mastered more than one. Starting back as a kid shooting by myself in my neighbor's backyard, I've had a lot of practice. I can shoot my jumper different ways, but mostly I shoot it jumping medium high and on the way up, soft and sort of flat.

In pro ball you look for your shot, but you have to be able to shoot from a lot of different places and a lot of different postures. This is where Elgin has been so outstanding. He is a more versatile shooter than any player at his peak. He has enormous strength, enabling him to go any place he wants. He has superb control of his body. And he has the greatest hands I've ever seen, with the greatest control of the ball. He can use spin, putting "English" on the ball, and play the ball off the backboards better than any other shooter. He is also the best at following a shot for a second shot. I honestly believe he deliberately misses some shots because he has angled them so they will come off where he can follow the shot in, grab the rebound, and be in a better position to score than he was the first time. Elgin always has had tremendous desire to score.

Elgin isn't the greatest pure shooter. He's seldom had one of the better shooting percentages among forwards in the league. But then, of course, he's always taken more difficult shots than anyone else. To me pure shooting is the art of just standing out there on the court and pumping it through. It has nothing to do with getting loose from your man or the quickness of your move. Adrian Smith, a guard, is the best pure shooter I've seen in the league, I think, although Oscar and Hal Greer are also very good. Jerry Lucas is the best pure shooter among forwards I've seen.

Rick Barry, Dave Bing and Elvin Hayes, who respectively led the NBA in scoring in 1967, '68 and '69, are not great pure shooters, but they work their way to a lot of points.

Dave Bing is small but a great jumper. MALCOLM W. EMMONS

Barry is very quick for his size and an unusually good run-
ner. He goes straight for the basket beautifully. With his running ability and quickness, he is able to get free or get in
position to get off shots from difficult angles or under heavy
defensive pressure. He hustles very hard and he *is* a good
shooter. The league lost a lot when he left to join the American Basketball Association. He should be a very fine player
and a tremendous scorer for many years. Hayes is agile for a
big man and has a good touch.

Bing's big asset is his quickness. He's even quicker than
Barry, which he has to be because he's not nearly as big. He's
small, but he's an unusually great jumper, which adds inches
to him. And he is a good shooter, too. When he first came
into this league he seemed very unsure of himself, but he
has learned very quickly. He really knows how to play now,
and he's very poised and relaxed. It's almost impossible to
bother him. He's improved tremendously and he has an opportunity to be one of the really great players.

There is hardly a good two-handed set-shooter or hook-
shooter left in the league. But there are a lot of kids who
shoot one-handed running all over the court like no one
before ever could shoot any way.

Twenty years ago Bob Feerick led the NBA in shooting
with 34 percent. A guy shooting like that today would have
trouble surviving the first out in pre-season camp. Bill Sharman is regarded as the best of the modern shooters, but he
used to shoot only about 40 or 42 percent, which wouldn't
be good enough today. It was a slower game then, too, and
outside shooters had more opportunity to get off clean shots.
The guys of the past just couldn't shoot with the kids of
today, and the kids of today get better every year.

Even the big centers of the past, guys like George Mikan
and Alex Groza who shot in close and got a lot of rebound buckets and tap-ins, didn't hit 50 percent when they
played. This league was 14 years old before anyone hit
50 percent of his shots and that 50 percenter was Wilt. That

happened in 1961, my first season in the league. Wilt usually
hits well above 50 percent of his shots from the field. In
1967, when he shot about half as often as he had in previous
years, he actually hit 68 percent of his shots. But you can't
give awards for pure shooting to fellows of his size who practically drop the ball in. Among centers, Clyde Lovellette was
actually a much better all-around shooter than Wilt. Mel
Counts is an exceptional outside shooter for a big center.

Wilt is so tall, so heavy, and so strong that when he wants
to shoot it is practically impossible to stop him from forcing
his way in close and dropping the ball in. It takes an exceptional defensive center, such as Russell, to stop him.
Mainly, Russell tries to prevent Wilt from getting his best
position. But Wilt does have a good touch with a fall-away
shot, though that moves him away from the basket and out of
position for rebounds. In practice he's deadly with this.

The tipoff on Wilt is that he's only been above 60 percent
from the free throw line once and he's been as low as 44
percent from there. Some seasons he's shot more accurately
from the field than from the foul line. He's actually a better
shooter from the field, mainly because he's more confident.
The fans don't hoot at him when he is shooting from the
field the way they do when he's shooting from the foul line.
He's failed at the free throw line so much he's psychologically
tied up in knots when he walks up there. He's fine in practice,
but terrible in games.

Shooting from the free throw line is not a difficult proposi-
tion. You need concentration and you need rhythm. You develop rhythm in practicing the same shot over and over again.
You're always standing in the same place, the basket is always in the same place, no one is defending you, and no
one is moving. I believe in shooting the same shot from the
free throw line that you shoot best from the field, because
it's the one you practice the most and have the most confidence in. In my case, I don't jump, of course, but I use the
same sort of one-handed motion. Hal Greer actually jumps.

I believe in shooting the same shot from the free throw line you shoot best from the field. Although I don't jump, I use the same sort of one-handed motion I do on my jump shot, as I show here in practice. I hold the ball on my full hand, cock it way back, come through with my elbow pointed toward the basket, let the ball roll off my finger tips and follow through by uncocking my wrist all the way down. WEN ROBERTS

You can shoot underhanded, too. It doesn't matter, so long as you have grooved your motion and rhythm in practice.

There are fellows who can hit 100 or 200 free throws in a row, and go around giving exhibitions to prove it, but they can concentrate because they're not tired from having played a game, and they're not bruised up from having been banged around in that game, and they're not choked up by knowing the game may hang on their shots. Under NBA pressure, Bill Sharman and Dolph Schayes were the best foul-shooters I ever saw. Oscar, Larry Costello, and Adrian Smith have been excellent, too.

The more you drive, the more you shoot from anywhere, the more chances you get at the free throw line, and so the more chances you get for points. It's very important to take advantage of this. I have, that's for sure.

Many good players don't know when to shoot. Hesitate and you're lost. If I don't have a shot, I'll lay the ball off. The important thing is to take only the shots you can hit a good percentage of the time. What's a good percentage? About half. I try to take only good percentage shots. I force a few shots. In Elgin's best year, he hit 45 percent of his shots. A couple of years he hit just about 40 percent. But he keeps banging away because he knows he's got a better chance of pulling a shot off and collecting points than most.

Elg averages about 25 shots a game. Dave Bing averages about 24, Oscar about 22. I average about 21. Still, I worry about shooting too much. I remember one night against St. Louis when my mother was at the game with my wife. Maybe I was showing off. Anyway, I was hot. I kept shooting and I must have had 30 points at halftime. In the dressing room, I thought the guys were looking at me funny, like maybe they thought I was shooting too much and they didn't like it. So, I stopped shooting. We won the game, so it was OK. But if we had lost, maybe it would have been because I stopped shooting, so it would have been my fault.

There have been a lot of times when I've stopped shoot-ing, and some of these times it has cost us games. It is very hard for me to keep shooting when I'm cold. Some guys don't give a darn, but I do. I really suffer because I know I'm letting the team down. If someone else has a hot hand, it's fine—I can stop shooting. You always feed the hot man. In my years with the Lakers, this has been one of our problems. They always fed Elg and me, no matter who was hot. But usually if Elg and I are cold and don't score, we lose. So we have to keep shooting and hope we warm up. Whenever I stop shooting, the coach usually gets on me.

This is a team game. All that counts is winning. I have to play both ends of the court and do other things besides shooting if I'm to do my job, but the main part of my job is getting us points. To do this, I have to shoot. I'm sure the guys realize it and accept it.

This whole business of balance in sports is overrated. A key man or two carries every team in every sport. They say Boston wins on balance, but take away Russell and the Celtics lose. He needs help. We all need help. But we're the key men and we know it. I figure I have to try to get up for every game and go all out every game. I have to set an example and lift the guys.

As the games go along, the harder things get, the better I like it. The challenge seems to lift me up. I know if we get beat, the writers and fans will look at me for the reason we lost. If we lose, I lose. It's what I've got to live with. It's OK. I'm used to it.

All athletes hate the term "choke up" more than any other. It is a cruel thing to say of a man and too often it is said carelessly. I hit more than my share of big baskets, but I blow some too. When I blow one, should I be called a choke-up? I don't think so. But I do think, to be brutally honest, that there are athletes in all sports who choke up under pressure. All athletes are different. Some are better than others, smarter, faster, stronger, tougher. And some respond to the big moment better than others. There are very fine basketball players in the NBA who avoid the big moments, who don't want the ball in the clutch, who don't want the responsibility, who are scared of failing. We don't expect them to come through. Sometimes it seems you can see their pants shaking when they have to shoot a big one.

I don't think there are choke-up teams. Every team has some players who come through in the clutch and some who don't. When you say a certain team chokes, you're being unfair to the players on that team who don't choke. But there are teams who don't have enough players who come through in the clutch, and so, as a team, they don't come through in the clutch very often.

The more you come through, the more you're apt to keep coming through. Confidence is a lot of this game or any game. If you don't think you can, you won't. The teams that strung together championships like the Yankees in baseball a few years back, the Packers in football, the Celtics in basketball— they had this confidence. They came through and kept coming through.

I have a reputation of being at my best when it counts the most. This is a lovely reputation to have, and I'm proud of it. It puts a lot of pressure on me, but I thrive on pressure. It excites me and brings out the best in me. When it comes to the clutch, I want the ball, I want to make the shot. I want it bad. I don't think anyone else has as good a chance of making it as I do. I know I can make it. I think others have confidence in me, which gives me confidence in myself.

Sometimes I've been called "Mr. Clutch." It has a silly sound to it, like "Superman" or "Captain Marvel" or something. I'm not superman or Captain Marvel. I'm just a guy, flesh and blood, nervous, scared to death sometimes, who has found he can put a basketball into a basket pretty easily and who has found he can do it best when it is important. This is a very nice thing. It's not discovering a cure for disease or pulling people out of burning buildings, but it's what I do and it's very nice for me to be able to do it well.

One day one of my sons came to me and asked me why I

Philadelphia's Hal Greer is practically leaning on me, forcing me to fall away a little to pop a jumper. WEN ROBERTS

was called "Mr. Clutch." I didn't know what to say to him.
I tried to explain it to him, simply and modestly. I said I
didn't especially like the term, though I know it was meant
well. It was embarrassing, but it was a very nice moment
having to explain to your son why someone says something
so flattering about you.

All kids want to grow up to hit home runs in the ninth
inning. I did. You don't think about it during the games.
They move too fast. But you live with it and it's always inside you. It gives me pride in myself. I know what I am and
what I'm not. I'm a good pro basketball player. Perhaps
that's the most important thing I am. But I'm many other
things, too.

When I'm off the court, I sometimes wish people would talk less about basketball.

11
Life at the Top

When I joined the Lakers, Bob Short, a Minneapolis business-man, was the owner. He was not making much money out of basketball and he was very reluctant to put much money back into it. When we were moved to L.A., Short became an absentee owner, which is a bad thing. There was never any-one on hand to make the ultimate decisions. Still, we prospered, and when Jack Kent Cooke bought the team in 1965, Short was paid more than five million dollars. That was a lot more than anyone had been paying for pro basketball franchises and it was considered much more than the L.A. franchise was worth at that time, but Mr. Cooke had the money, he was willing to spend it, he was very anxious to get a pro sports franchise, and he probably knew it would be worth more in a few years.

Bob Short seemed to blame me for every loss and I resented it. Anyway, we never got along very well, but, fortunately, we never had to have a lot to do with each other. I like Jack Kent Cooke very much, I know he likes me, and we get along very well. A lot of people don't like Jack. He's a controversial person. But I can only say how I see him. He's always treated me well. He's always been friendly and open with me. He's always been fair. He's never gone back on his word. I see how successful he is and I respect him very much.

Mr. Cooke is a Canadian who started out with nothing, selling soap and encyclopedias door to door. He went into broadcasting and publishing and was a millionaire by the time he was in his early 30s. He once owned the Toronto Maple Leafs' minor league baseball team and he later bought a fourth of the Washington Redskins' pro football team, which he still has. He moved to the United States and began a new empire in the television business, installing and renting cable facilities in areas where there would otherwise be poor reception. He's a millionaire many times over, I guess.

Being a self-made man, Mr. Cooke may find it a little hard to delegate authority. He is used to doing things himself, his own way. He is a perfectionist and very demanding. He works very hard and expects his employees to work very hard. A lot of people seem to come and go quickly in his organization, but I get the impression that if you do your job, Jack will treat you well.

He is definitely the boss of his businesses and his ball club. He oversees his managers, coaches, and players. He makes a lot of the decisions. He is in the spotlight more than most owners. A lot of people object to this. But he is a colorful, extroverted person. If I owned a club, I'd want to run it actively, too.

At the Sports Arena, Jack and his wife and friends used to sit at midcourt in a row of seats that was spread along the side of the court. From here, he made himself heard, rooting very hard. When Rudy LaRusso was traded during the 1966-67 season, Rudy said that Jack put too much pressure on his players with personal contact and that he was ruining morale.

Athletes are very sensitive and I'm sure Rudy and some others objected to Mr. Cooke's rooting. But Rudy, whom I like and respect, didn't sound off until he was traded, so you have to see that he was upset, and saying something he otherwise might not have said. Maybe he meant it. But I, personally, have never felt it.

I'm flattered by Mr. Cooke's rooting. I'm pleased when he stops by the dressing room to say kind words to me. And he never says any other kind. He has never criticized me directly. The fact is, he seldom even comes in the Laker dressing room after games. And in the Forum he and his family and friends sit so far away we're not even aware of them.

Perhaps Mr. Cooke treats me better than he does some others, though I haven't seen him treat anyone badly. I think Jack does admire successful people and star athletes and it is something to feel admiration coming from a man like this. Mrs. Cooke is a lovely, warm woman. They have two married sons who are active in Jack's businesses. Jack loves sports, and he seems to devote almost all of his time to sports.

After he bought the Lakers, he landed the new franchise of the National Hockey League in Los Angeles. No one thought he would get it. There were many other wealthy and influential bidders, including Dan Reeves, who owns the Los Angeles Rams pro football team and was running the L.A. minor league hockey team. But Mr. Cooke is a very persuasive salesman and he landed the team, the Kings, who began play during the 1967-68 season.

At the time Mr. Cooke was seeking the franchise, he could not get together on a contract he liked with the Coliseum Commission, which operated the Sports Arena, where the Lakers played. As part of his bid for the hockey team, he promised to build his own indoor arena. Few felt he would really do it, since the Sports Arena was and still is a fine big, beautiful building, less than ten years old. However, Jack usually does what he sets out to do. Midway in the 1967-68 season, he opened his Forum.

It cost $16,250,000. It is more beautiful and bigger than the Sports Arena and obviously newer. Where the Sports Arena is located in a rather depressed area of southwest Los Angeles, the Forum is located in suburban Inglewood, adjacent to the Hollywood Park horse-race track. It is by far the finest building I've ever played in, very fancy and plush and comfortable.

Not that I had any complaints with the Sports Arena. But Jack has lured a lot of ice shows and circuses and things like that to his new building and he brought his two teams there. The Los Angeles Stars of the American Basketball Association, who started in Anaheim, play in the Sports Arena.

Actually, I wish the ABA well. If the league survives, it will give the NBA competition and assure more money for the players, although the rookies, who will have their choice between two teams in two leagues, will benefit the most.

I signed with Bob Short for $15,000 and no bonus my first season in the NBA. Elvin Hayes signed for ten times that much for the 1968-69 season with San Diego in the NBA, and he was not a much bigger star in college ball than I was, though he is much bigger physically. I can't even guess what Lew Alcindor really got when he turned pro. He figures to be another Wilt or Russell and those kind are worth a lot of money.

The minimum salary in the NBA is $10,000. I do not believe many are making this. Most are making much more. The average regular in the NBA probably gets $25,000, although long-term and bonus contracts such as have been given Russell or Chamberlain or rookies like Hayes run very high and make it very difficult to figure an average accurately. There are a few making around $100,000 a year. I am one. I am sure Elgin, Oscar, Wilt, and Russell are others.

Reportedly, Russell is making around $200,000 a season. I'd guess he is. Of course he is in a special category because he not only has brought his team to so many championships, but now is the coach, too. Whatever he's paid, I'm sure he's worth it. Reportedly Wilt is making around this figure, too. When Mr. Cooke acquired Wilt from Philadelphia in the summer of 1968, he had to go very high to get his name on a long-term contract. I understand Wilt is a very tough man to bargain with. But we each have our own idea of our worth.

Pro athletes are the most spoiled people in the world. The big ones are almost indispensable so they sometimes all but blackmail the owners with their demands. I don't believe in this. I don't bring a lawyer to contract sessions. Mr. Cooke doesn't have his laywer with him. Of course, he's a sharper businessman than I am, but I know what I'm worth as a basketball player.

I may get tougher over the bargaining table, but Mr. Cooke and I haven't had much trouble. I've risen steadily every season. I believe in long-term, two- or three-year contracts, and I've gotten them. I do want more money. It is possible Wilt is worth more than I am, but I don't think he's worth more than twice as much. I only ask that I be treated fairly.

The top pro athletes are very well paid. I'm well aware of this. If this were a time when pro basketball players played for $7,500 or $10,000 a season, I'd still be playing anyway. But it is a time when teams are making more money and can afford to pay their players more, and I want my share, as does every other athlete. Our time in this salary bracket is very limited, and we have to make it while we can.

I'm fortunate to be playing in Los Angeles, where the club is doing well. But I don't think a player should be penalized if he's playing in a smaller town on a club that isn't doing as well. The player has no choice as to which club he lands with. If the club owner can't afford to stay in business, let him get out of the business. If he can't afford to pay the athlete what he's worth, let the athlete go to a club that can. The owner will pay as little as he can get away with in every case. The athlete has to look out for himself.

The pro athlete makes good money, makes good contacts, makes a name for himself. He has a marvelous opportunity to make a place for himself in life. Not everyone takes advantage of it. A lot of them go their own way, live high, make foolish investments. If that's the way they want to travel, fine. It's their lives, not mine. A lot of them had nothing when they went into sports. If they come out of it with nothing, at least they had all that went in between, which they otherwise might not have had.

When you're a name athlete making a lot of money, everyone wants to sell you something or get you to invest in something—restaurants and bars mostly, but a lot of other things as well. Some of them may be very good things, but I'm very cautious. I never had much and I don't ever want to want for anything again. I like to see the money in the bank. What I have invested in has been mostly in real estate and stocks.

Certainly, some things are more satisfying than making money. However, one of my goals has always been to get so well fixed financially I would not have to worry about having a comfortable life and sending my kids through college and things like that after I retire. It's maybe not the sort of thing I should say, but the fact is that for a long time I've kind of thought that when I retire I might like to retire completely, just hunt and fish and enjoy life. I don't want to have to punch a clock for a living. If something comes along that I like and am good at, fine.

Actually, were I playing in New York, my name would mean a lot more. For one thing, people in Los Angeles are not as knowledgeable about basketball as they are in many other cities, especially in the East and especially in New York. I have felt that the people who should know better, the people who write about sports, could have done a better job of distributing the plaudits in pro basketball than they have in Los Angeles. Many times I have gotten too much credit for scoring a lot of points. Other times I have not gotten enough credit for a steal or a pass. It is the little things that turn basketball games around, but too often these are overlooked in favor of the obvious things.

Of course, what the reporters write is their business, but it does gripe me as a player. I don't enjoy reading about our games the way I feel I would like to. Possibly this is partly my fault because I don't open up to writers and tell them what I think has happened in a game as much as I should, but I figure my job is playing the game and their job is analyzing it.

I'm not really flashy and I've never felt I got the sort of credit I deserve for what I do. This isn't easy for me to say, but it's what I really feel and I don't want to pull any punches. Take my teammate, Elg. Besides being great, Elgin is also flashy. Throw in his dramatic comeback from serious injury and you have an unbeatable combination. It is not his doing, but it is a fact that he gets more applause from the press and fans than I do, and I'd be less than honest if I didn't admit I was a little jealous about it.

It goes a little deeper than that. I'll give you an example, which is a sort of personal confession. When Elgin scored his 15,000th point in an NBA game, the club was ready for it, and they stopped the game and presented him the ball, and the fans gave him a standing ovation, and later they mounted the ball on a trophy for him. He deserved it. It was beautiful. And I was moved by it.

I knew when I was about to score my 15,000th point. My wife and I were all excited about it. I left for the game anticipating a beautiful moment. Well, I scored it and nothing happened. The moment came and went. No one did anything about it. No one said anything. No one wrote anything. Maybe it's ego, but I don't think I'm really vain. It was disappointing and it hurt me. My wife gave me a trophy, which was very nice, but not the same.

If I had played my career in New York, I'm sure my stature as a ballplayer would have been greater and would endure longer. I'd certainly have the opportunity for more side benefits than I do now. But then I'd get less than I do now if I played in Milwaukee or Cincinnati or Detroit. It doesn't really bother me a lot, however. It did for a while, but I find I'm well compensated for what I do.

Ballplayers are offered various amounts of money to endorse various items. I don't take as much of this action as I could. I'm just careful. I got into something once with putting my name on a basketball for a sporting goods firm and I didn't feel it was being handled well and I got into a hassle about it and just dropped it. I don't need the headaches.

Some people just want to take advantage of you for their own personal gain. So I'm very selective. I have a very good arrangement with Jantzen, the sports clothes people. I'm sure you've seen my picture along with Frank Gifford, Paul Hornung, Terry Baker, and a number of other athletes modeling bathing suits or things like that in exotic locales. On location trips, my wife and I have gotten to Europe, South America, Hawaii, and other places, all expenses paid. It's very nice.

I've also done well with Karl's Shoes, endorsing a basketball shoe. There are one or two other things. They come and they go. Something is always on the fire. If it's going to take much of me, I don't want it. I don't have the time and I don't want to take my concentration away from basketball. Some athletes get so deeply involved in sidelines that their play suffers, and I don't want that.

I have an interest in a summer camp. There are a number of other boys' camps and basketball camps that I'm committed to. Some take more time than I want to give them. But I enjoy working with kids and I feel an obligation to some friends and fellow athletes who run the camps. On the other hand, my name has been used on some which I have no connection with, which is annoying.

I am often asked to speak at banquets and special affairs and club meetings. I do some of this, though not as much as some athletes. I don't mind it, but I just don't have the time. Sometimes they expect you to drive 50 or 100 miles between games just to put in an appearance. When I first got into the NBA, I did more of this, but it wore me out.

The appearances I do make, I enjoy. I don't mind signing autographs for kids. I know when I was a kid I'd have loved to have gotten Ted Williams or Stan Musial to sign an autograph for me. I know what hero worship is, even if I know the heroes aren't always all that the kids think they are.

I have the reputation of being the All-American boy. To some extent, I guess I am. Certainly, I was a lot more so at one time. I'm sort of a straight character, kind of dull. I don't swing a whole lot. I'm devoted to my sport. I'm devoted to my wife and kids. I don't pop off and I have no skeletons in my closet.

If I'm something special on the court, I'm really nothing special off it. It's no good for me and I'd just as soon I didn't, but I take a drink now and then. I try to be nice to everyone, but there are people I don't like. Most people are nice to me, but I'm sure if they got to know me, some of them wouldn't like me.

I'm not all puffed up about myself, but I have an ego just like everyone else. I get cross with my wife sometimes and I yell at the kids sometimes. I'm too moody and too quiet and I'm not the easiest person in the world to live with. I'm just a guy like other guys, no more perfect than anyone else.

Actually, a lot of the straight stuff is because I do have this reputation and I feel I ought to try to live up to it. It's hard sometimes. It's sort of like being in a straight-jacket and once in a while I get fed up with it. Sometimes I think I'd like to go off on a tear just to be rid of my image. But I don't really want to. And I don't have the stomach for it.

It's a nice image for my sons, but I don't feel really worthy of it and I'd just as soon be done with it. I can't do anything about it. Kids and dogs like me.

My wife Jane and I have three children now, all sons—David, who was born in 1960, Michael, who was born in 1962, and Mark, who was born in 1963. We also have a springer spaniel, Fluffy. We live in a nice, but modest house in West L.A. We've lived there since 1963. During the summer of 1968 we almost bought a much more elaborate place in the San Fernando Valley, but finally decided against it. We're basically conservative people. We'll move one of these days, although we know the neighborhood and like our neighbors.

We're a very close family. I'm happy about that and I think I've tried for this because when I was a kid mine wasn't a close family that did things together or could talk to one another easily. Jane and I are very close. She understands me and puts up with a lot from me. I'm sensitive and I suf-

A family portrait, 1968. Jane, the kids, left to right: Mark, Michael and David. WEN ROBERTS

fer a lot during the season, but she gives me the sympathy I want, and caters to me, and leaves me alone when I want to be left alone. I can't imagine anyone else putting up with me the way she does. And she does a marvelous job with the boys.

My sons are the happiest kids I've ever known. They've never seen the other side of life. They've never had it tough. I worry about that sometimes. But what should I do, abandon them in a ghetto for a year? I guess they've either got the right stuff in them or they don't. We try to be strict with them, and we don't give them everything they want, but we do spoil them. And since I'm away from them so much, traveling during the season and all, I try to make up for it by giving them a lot of attention when I'm home. We go places together. Jane always sees that they're well dressed and clean.

They're just becoming aware that their father is a big basketball star. I guess it's kind of nice for them, but I don't
think it means a whole lot to them yet. I do know that I
got worn out lugging home photos of myself and autograph-
ing them for David. I thought he was giving them away to
his friends at school. Then I found out he was selling them
for a penny apiece. When one of his teachers sent a note home
that he was spending all his time taking orders, I put a stop
to it.

I don't know if they'll be basketball players. I'll be pleased
and proud if they are. They might have inherited some of
their old man's talent, but I can't picture them practicing
alone for hours until after dark in some neighbor's backyard.
It doesn't matter. I just want them to do whatever they
find they want to do. I only hope they're serious enough
about it to go at it hard. Right now, they swim and ride
bikes and play ball. Southern California is a nice place to
raise kids.

They're good boys and I'm proud of them.

Jane and I don't go out a whole lot. We're home people.
And we don't have a lot of free time, especially during the
season. I'm the original visiting fireman. I love all sports
and when the Lakers aren't playing, I'm apt to be watching
the Kings play hockey or the Dodgers or Angels play baseball. I've always got the radio or television on to some game
or other. I'm interested in all sports and I like being around
athletes. It's a sort of private club and I'm a member.

Sometimes when I'm out, though, I wish I weren't an athlete. I don't mind it when I'm speaking at some affair, but
I do when we're at a private party or at a restaurant or a
show and people keep talking sports in general and basketball in particular.

We get asked the same questions over and over. Why
did you win? Why did you lose? How come you guys never
win the playoffs? How come Selvy took that shot? How do
you get along with Elgin? Now, how do you get along with

Wilt? What is Elgin like? What is Wilt like? What is the real Jack Kent Cooke like?

The same questions over and over. It's OK—I mean, let's face it, when I'm with another ball player, especially in another sport, I ask the same questions. It's OK until the questions get personal. Most people are nice, but some are nasty. When they start asking you about the club's operation or some controversy or some guy's love life, you pull away and shut up.

The fan letters from the kids are fine. Some of my happiest moments come from these. These kids are so sincere in their awe of you, so devoted to sports, so hungry for affection it gets to you. Maybe it's not true, but somehow you get the feeling they respect you for yourself, not just for your basketball.

Once in a while you get a nasty note. Why do you shoot so much? Why don't you pass to Baylor more? Why do the Lakers choke up against Boston? It's sad that some people have so much meanness in them. Some people, not many. Face to face, most people are not at all mean. Maybe they're intimidated by you, but most people are nice in person. I sometimes wonder where those people are who write some of the letters and do some of the yelling at games.

It's nice being known, but you can have too much of a good thing. You don't enjoy being stared at when you're shoveling soup down your mouth in a restaurant. You don't enjoy being followed into the men's room and asked for an autograph. It is annoying to feel you shouldn't go some places or be seen taking a drink in public because of your image.

My main complaint is that I wish I could be myself more and be taken for myself more. Maybe I'm nothing special off the court, but I would like to feel that I'd be welcome some places even if I weren't a good outside shooter. I guess it's worse if you're a singer or a musician or something. People are always asking them to perform at parties. At least no one asks me to pop in a jumper. But I do wish sometimes they'd talk to me about something besides basketball.

It's very hard to know if people want to be with you because they like you and like some of the things you like or because you're a basketball star. You get suspicious, which is sad. Also, there are very few people other than athletes whose circumstances are like ours. As a result of all of these things, Jane and I don't have many close friends, and those friends we do have are mostly other athletes and their wives.

We were very close to Terry Baker and his wife until the Rams traded him out of town. We also were very close to Darrall and Susan Imhoff before the Lakers traded him to Philadelphia. I went to a lot of games with Gale Goodrich, but then he went to Phoenix. I go to games with Rod Hundley a lot.

I've been very fortunate that I've never been traded. Mr. Cooke has said I never will be and at this point I don't believe I will be. Professional sports is a tough enough life as it is, but being bounced with your family from one town to another must make it ten times worse.

It is hard enough on those who are left behind. A team is a family. If it's a happy family, it has a good chance of being a winner. I think the bosses of teams neglect this aspect of things. The more changes you make in personnel, the more you disrupt the family. If you have improved your team, fine. But if you have made a change just to make a change, the chances are you have hurt morale.

In some ways, the off-seasons are harder on me than the seasons. Of course, I don't have the pressure of having to play big games. But it does seem that there are so many demands on my time that I'm always flying in and out of town, always living in hotels and out of suitcases all summer, and very often I don't know if I'm coming or going. At least during the season I have a strict schedule to follow and I have plenty of excuses to beg out of things I don't want to do.

12
A Band of Gypsies

Basketball is my life. For some players, it's just a small part of their lives. For me it's the biggest part, aside from my family. I live from game to game. Almost every off-day we have, and we don't seem to have many, we practice. As long as the season is, I love practice. Obviously, I'm a real oddball. But the reason is it's one time I can fool around with a basketball in my hand. I love the game and it's fun to relax with it. I practice hard. I work at the game in practice. But I goof off, too, kidding around with the guys.

On game days, I can't wait for the game to begin. It's a long day. I usually get up about 9 or so in the morning and have breakfast around 9:30. I skip lunch. I eat my pre-game meal about 3:30, about four or five hours before the tip-off. I'm a steak man, but very often I just have some fruit and cottage cheese or a small salad, or maybe just a can of Nutriment or Metrecal. I have a nervous stomach. As the games approach, I don't feel like eating.

I try to take a nap before my pre-game meal. I got out of the habit of taking a nap after the meal, as many athletes do, and I hate to change my routine because I'm sort of superstitious. If I do something and we win, I'm apt to keep doing that until we lose.

The hours pass slowly. At home I look for chores to do or errands to run. On the road I take walks or play cards or

We used to kid Darrall Imhoff about being traded for Chamberlain.
Then he was. UPI

watch TV or snap at my roomie. I get wound up. I wear
myself out thinking about the game.

I'm used to the traveling by now, so I don't mind it too
much. The change in time busts me up a little bit, but I'm
all busted up on game days anyway. I dislike some cities

we hit. I'm not too keen on Philadelphia, Baltimore, or Detroit, for example. These are old cities. The weather is usually bad during the basketball season. You never seem to see any trees or grass. I'm sure there's more to these cities than I see coming and going. I do enjoy visiting Boston, San Francisco, and San Diego. Obviously, I like California. Boston is old and has bad weather, but it has some sort of charm that gets to me. New York is always an exciting place to visit, but we don't have time to do it up right.

I'm a bad one to turn to for tips on the hot spots. I can tell you which hotels have the softest chairs in the lobby and provide the cleanest towels.

Home or away, I cut out for the arena as soon as possible. The sooner I get there, the nearer the game seems. The nearer the game seems, the more tied up in knots I get. I'm not as bad as I used to be. I don't need as many pills. I've been this way before. I know the road. But it's always big to me. Always big. I'm never relaxed. Not even after the whistle blows and the game begins. But it's better then. I'm doing it then. I'm moving and getting belted around and muttering to myself and I don't have to think about anything else but the game, which is my game.

After the game, if my stomach will take it, I may grab a sandwich. It takes me a while to unwind. I see a lot of late shows. And late late shows. And later-than-that shows. I'm an expert on Shirley Temple's movie career. Finally, sleep. I'm a heck of a sleeper if we've won. If we've lost, forget it. I'm not good at anything when we lose.

The family makes it easier. I mean the basketball family. We're very close. I don't mean we tell each other our troubles. Outsiders seem to think we know everything about the other players. We don't. I probably don't know as much about Elg as some writers do. To some extent, we hold ourselves apart from one another. In fact, even on the same team we're competitive. It's a hard sort of pressure we face —our jobs on the line every season, every game, really. People who aren't athletes don't have to perform in public 100 times a year and have the pluses and minuses added up in awful detail in box scores and lists of statistics all season long.

What we do is we feel for each other. We know what we're doing. We know the box scores don't tell the whole story. We know sometimes the number of points you score has no relation to the game you played. We play the game, so we know what it is. When a guy plays a bum game and the writers come around to congratulate him for having played a great game, we smile, but we hold it inside. When a guy gets cut or traded, we feel for him. But when he's letting the team down, we're angry with him. Usually we don't pop off about it. We keep it in the family.

The monotony of the long season gets to you sometimes, especially on the road. We relieve it ridiculing one another. We relieve it complaining. Like guys in the Army, we go at one another and everyone around us all the time, looking for laughs.

The guys call me "Zeke." They also call me "Tweety" or "Tweety-Bird." I guess it comes partly from my thin, high voice and partly from my thin, long legs. Who knows? Most of the time, you have no idea when the names start and where they come from. Rudy LaRusso has always been "Deuce." Jim Krebs was "Boomer." Darrall Imhoff has been "Hammer Head" or "Headquarters" or "Astrodome" or just plain "Dome," all because he has a large head.

The guys used to go up to "Dome" and look in his ears to check the weather for that night's game. Imhoff always loved to stuff the ball. One night in pre-game practice he went up to stuff it and blew it. "Deuce" and Elgin ran off the court and perched in front-row seats begging "Dome" to show 'em that trick shot again.

One night one of our former players, Henry Finkel, who was with San Diego, scored 47 points off the "Dome." Poor Darrall never heard the end of it. He was reminded that he had been New York's center when Wilt scored his 100. "Hey,

Dome, I want to play against you," the guys needled. Imhoff kept muttering it wasn't his fault. I remember he said, "When I left that game, Wilt had 28. When I went back in, he had 78." He swore Finkel would never get another basket against him. The next time they played, Finkel got 40.

Gale Goodrich, who was called "Stumpy," is short and has a lot of shots blocked. The guys always used to kid him about being blocked into the bleachers or driven ten feet down into the court. They used to say he held the record for the longest line drive home runs ever hit off a basketball guard.

Even non-players are not exempt. Frank O'Neill, our trainer, is "Little Hawg" or just plain "Hoggy" or "Piggy." We sneak ears of corn into his bed. One night we sneaked a skeleton into his closet. Like a doctor, he doesn't want any-one to touch his little black bag. So we steal it, hide it, put all sorts of things in it.

Killing time, we pick teams of the five worst players in the league or the five ugliest players. There are always a million rumors. I'm supposed to be the world's champion rumor-monger. I'm a sucker for every interesting story and can't resist passing it on. We make up our own trades and pass them on to the other players and writers.

"Hey, Elg, you've just been traded for Oscar Robertson. But Cooke had to throw in half-a-million dollars," one of us might say. Or, "Hey, Dome, you just went for Wilt." So it actually happened: Dome and other players and money for Wilt. I was in Spain when I heard about it. I couldn't believe it. So many players have been coming and going, you can't kid about trades any more.

Nothing is to be believed. Nothing is ever to be believed. "Did you see that officiating? Can you believe it?" the guys ask one another after a game. Or "Can you believe that Rodgers? How can he get 30 in a game?" or "Can you believe this weather?" Or "Can you believe this schedule?"

One night we were waiting so long for our plane it wasn't to be believed. You get tired and you get punchy and you get silly. LaRusso walked into the airport shop and studied a stuffed animal that had a 50-dollar price tag on it. "I can't believe that lion is 50 dollars," Deuce said.

Boomer said, "It's a tiger, not a lion."

"Let's see," Deuce said, picking it up. Suddenly he fell to the floor, wrestling violently with the toy. "Get an elephant gun," he screamed, while people ran up to see what all the commotion was about. Gingerly, Deuce replaced the animal. "I told you it was a lion," he said. "It got mad when I asked him if he was a tiger."

We broke up.

The next trip in, Deuce rushed back to the shop. "Let's have that lion," he said. The salesgirl handed it to him, pointing out that it was 50 dollars. "I don't want to buy it," Deuce said. "I want to fight it. I want a rematch."

We don't always act like adults, you see. It's a game we play, so we act like kids sometimes.

Once on a flight, Deuce asked how much we'd offer to hit him with a cream pie. We offered two bucks. Deuce accepted. We got up the dough. Howie Jolliff did the honors. He slammed Deuce in the face with the pie. He did it so enthusiastically that pie sprayed all over everyone, including Schaus, sitting several rows back. Fred hit the roof.

Some of the guys get scared on air trips. We make jokes about it, but it's not funny. Fear never is. Some guys break out in a cold sweat every time the plane does a little dance. If you fly as much as we have to, you have to sweat through a lot of little dances. I've been uneasy myself. Even Elgin, who is such a cool cat, gets nervous. Rod Hundley always said Elgin flew with one hand on his armrest and one hand on his wallet. He grips the armrest so hard sometimes it begins to come apart in sawdust. One of the guys will come up to him and ask, "Hey, Elg, how about a chorus of 'Nearer My God To Thee'?"

One thing about being up there is that it brings out the honesty in guys. When we get some character who lies a lot, we wait until we get up in the air and then we ask him the key questions. It's amazing how reluctant they are to lie when they're up there. One guy used to insist he was five years younger than he really was. Flying aged him five years.

A lot of our trips are tough. One time we played in L.A. on a Friday night and had a game in Chicago the next night. There was a snowstorm in Chicago and they told us no planes were getting through. They didn't want to chance waiting until the morning, so they booked us on a flight that night to Minneapolis, figuring we could fly on to Chicago from there the next day. We got on the plane in Minneapolis at 8:30 in the morning without having more than orange juice and coffee and maybe a sweet roll.

Then when we got over Chicago, they wouldn't let us set down, so we had to fly on to Milwaukee. In Milwaukee, we just sat around. They kept telling us we'd leave any minute, but we never seemed to leave. Finally, we had to take a bus. We grabbed ham and cheese sandwiches and cardboard containers of milk from a box-lunch place and drove through the blizzard to Chicago. We arrived late. And we played one of the greatest games we played all season.

Sports can be very unpredictable. Lots of times you feel good and play bad. Other times, you're sick or tired or hungry and just don't really want to play and you go out there and everything works for you. You win and lose games sometimes when you least expect to. No one can figure it out. If you could, you'd make a fortune.

Another time we played a great game in Chicago on a Sunday afternoon after a real tough trip in. We'd played in Cincinnati on Saturday night. The weather was bad between Cincy and Chicago, so they put us up in a hotel and told us they'd call us at 6:30 the next morning. They called us two hours late and told us the planes were grounded, so we'd have to take a train.

The train was late. As we approached Chicago, they told us we'd have to get dressed on the train so we could be ready to play the minute we got to Chicago. Can you imagine six-foot-plus characters getting taped in train compartments with their feet sticking out in the narrow isles? Somehow we got dressed and stepped off the train in uniforms and basketball shoes—up to our knees in snow.

We managed to get taxis. The game was being played at the Ampitheater, which is next to the stockyards. That's where the Democratic National Convention was held in 1968. It smells pretty bad. It's also a pretty cold barn. The temperature was 10 degrees outside and 20 below inside. There were about 1,000 people in the place. No one wanted to play. No one wanted to see us play. It was ridiculous. So we played a tremendous game.

The thing I remember best about that trip was the breakfast one of the guys grabbed at the train terminal. He asked the waitress for root beer—hot. She didn't believe him. But he was serious. He liked hot root beer for breakfast. I remember he had scrambled eggs, whole wheat toast, and three glasses of hot root beer. He kept sending back the eggs because they were overdone. Finally, the waitress brought him eggs that were running all over the plate and that satisfied him. In Chicago he grabbed a hot dog and another hot root beer before the game. He played all right as I remember. He wasn't anything special as a player. But he was a special sort of person, that's for sure.

I'm very careful about what I eat. I just eat straight stuff, and not much of that. Sometimes I get on health food kicks. But nothing exotic. I'm too nervous. Some of these guys have guts of steel. I can remember one guy eating a big, fat, juicy pizza in the dressing rooms right before a championship game. I get sick just thinking about it, but I guess it's all in what you're used to. We all get used to making do on cheese sandwiches if necessary. We may get paid well, but there just isn't time to eat well a lot of the time.

I used to think Elgin was something special as an eater. It wasn't so much what he ate, but that he ate more of every-

Rudy LaRusso (with ball), Elg and I liked to have eating races.
LOS ANGELES LAKERS

thing. But as he's gotten older, he's been eating less. Of course, he's a big man, but that isn't always the key thing.

Elg is the fastest eater. A talent like this can be regarded pretty highly in the athletes' inner circle. Rudy LaRusso, Elg, and I used to have races. I mean we'd eat at our normal pace, but see who finished first because we were all proud of our speed with the knife and fork. There was no way we could keep up with Elgin. He'd eat more and faster than almost anyone. Food would just disappear off his plate. If you think he's a magician with a basketball, you should see him with a fork. He waves it over his plate and presto, it's empty.

Basketball players come and go and you live with a lot of different types if you hang around long enough. I remember one guy smelled bad. We used to kid him about it. We used to say that he couldn't use deodorant or after-shave lotion because he had this special problem and his skin would break out in a rash if he did. He took the kidding well, but he really did smell bad. Fortunately, he also played bad and wasn't around long.

We have had some bad characters from time to time. I remember one guy in particular, but I can't say too much about him because it couldn't be printed, even these days. Unlike most rookies, he came on strong. I remember we were playing some exhibitions in Honolulu and we were walking down the street and he goes up to a girl and hands her his room key and tells her he's one of the Lakers, baby, and if she wants to show up at 5:30, he'll be there, baby. Well, believe it or not, she showed up. Characters like this seem to get away with murder. But they usually don't last. He didn't.

We had another character on the Lakers who was a good player but a better boozer. He wasted away his talent. When he got drunk, he snored. I roomed with him one season and I tried to get to sleep nights before him so I could sleep. Once he began to snore, there was no hope unless you were way under.

I'd be sleeping and he'd come in about two in the morning with the early edition of the paper. He'd flip on all the lights and begin to rustle the morning paper, going through the box scores and telling me how everyone did the night before: "Hey, Jer, you asleep? Listen to what ol' Wilt did. Whatta you think happened in Philly?" And so on.

I'd fight it, but eventually I'd be wide awake. Then, he'd stagger to his feet and mutter something about being exhausted and fall on the bed with all his clothes on. Right away, he'd be dead to the world, snoring a ton. And I'd be laying there, grinding my teeth. I finally quit him. So did a lot of guys. Schaus couldn't figure out why no one would room with this character.

We have rules, but most guys bend them a little, if they don't plain break them. You only fine or suspend guys in extreme cases. After all, the hours we keep have to be sort of unusual. You finish up games at 11 at night or so. By the time you get back to a hotel it's close to midnight. Usually you want to eat something and want to unwind. You're supposed to be in bed by 1, but it's pretty hard even if you're not running around. Half the time, we're just getting on a plane at 1. You get into some city at 3 or 4 or 5 in the morning and have to sleep during the day. It's pretty rough.

Some guys would rather stay up all night and sleep all day. They'd rather play their basketball games at the start of their day, which happens to be 8 at night, just like most people start to work a little while after they get up. It's a little tough to do your best at the end of a long day, after sitting around.

Rod Hundley was like that. It is no secret that Rod always has liked to live a little. Rudy LaRusso used to remark on how amazing it was that Rod's car started up all by itself every night at 11:30.

Rod likes to socialize and he's a good-looking guy with a gift of gab. We'd be going on a plane and one of the pretty stewardesses would ask him if he was a basketball player and he'd say, "You better believe it, baby; the best, the very best." And Rod really believed it, too. I think he wasted his talent some, however. But he's a funny guy and people like him.

One of the funniest guys in sports is Johnny Kerr, who is now coaching. I'm sorry I didn't get to play with Johnny, or under him, simply because he is an amusing person. A stewardess once wished him luck as he left a flight. He asked her how many stops she had to make yet on that flight. She said three. He said, "Good luck to you. You're the one who needs it."

John used to say he got to be an All-America at Illinois because he worked at the publicity office and would only send out his picture. He's always talking about the book he's going to write. Sometimes he says he's going to call it, "Ten Years in the Pivot without the Ball." But he also figured he might show a lady leaning up against a lamppost on the cover, call it "The Last Of The Great Hookers," and get it banned in Boston.

Once John and some players got on an elevator and a passenger remarked on the size of the fellows. "It's a jockey's convention," John explained. Coaching in Phoenix, John wound up with one of the Van Arsdale twins, Dick. The other one, Tom, was with Cincinnati. One day, John went to Dick and said, "Great news, we're close to swinging a deal for your brother. The only thing is, they want a lot." Dick said, "Gee, that'd really be wonderful. Who do they want?" And John said, "You."

"Darlin' " Dick Barnett was as funny as any player the Lakers have ever had. He was naturally funny. But he got offended when you said he was funny. He thought he was serious. When he got into a shooting slump, he said, "My jumper's on vacation." When he got hot, he said, "Vacation's over." After a great night's shooting, he greeted the press, "Gentlemen, I just don't know what the trouble is. I just can't seem to get my shooting average over 80 percent." When a teammate blew a big basket, Dick slid over to him and said softly, "Darlin', you got a touch like a blacksmith."

Lonely in his room, he would call a teammate and flip a pack of cards into the telephone mouthpiece: "Hey, darlin'," he'd say, "they're playing the national anthem." Or maybe he'd call Elg and say, "Elg, baby, the cards are here, where's your wallet?" Once when Schaus went around reminding the boys there'd be a bed check that night, Dick said, "Don't you worry, coach, darlin'. You come check. I guarantee you the bed will be there."

He's very proud of his peculiar shooting style. He goes around telling people, "I don't know who invented the jump shot, but I know who invented the fall-back shot."

Barnett was a fancy dresser, and Hot Rod Hundley, who was his roommate, recalls one morning when he woke up to find Barnett, dressed to the teeth and admiring himself in a full-length mirror. "Go on, Dick," he was saying. "Go on, darlin', don't let anything stop you. On to Wall Street, darlin'. On to the top."

Dick was very proud of the way he dressed. When he was on our team, he used to cross swords with Elgin, another fancy dresser. Studying Elgin he'd say, "Darlin', clothes may make the man, but men didn't make those duds."

Elgin would finger Dick's coat. "What race was he in?" he'd ask.

With Barnett gone, Elg remains the expert on clothing. Imhoff always bought wild ties. "Hey, Dome, you tryin' to hide something? Wouldn't it be better to just wear shirts?" Elg would ask. "Who's flag is that? Or is it one of those Berkeley LSD dreams?"

I had a green-checked coat I had worn ever since college. Elg really admired that coat. "That's a rather nice thing you have there, Tweety-Bird," he said. "Does it come in men's clothing, too?" I never wore it again.

One day when he was on leave from the Army, Elg turned up with some real elegant shoes. "How much did they cost?" I asked. He said 75 dollars. "Boy you can't beat those sales at the PX," I said.

Now that I think about it, I've never seen those shoes since.

Actually, Elg is the world champion long-distance, nonstop expert on everything. A plane takes off and Elg asks you what kind it is, tells you you're wrong, then tells you everything about it from the cost to the peak speed, from passenger capacity to fuel capacity. If he doesn't know the facts, he makes them up.

No one tops him. If you saw a four-car crash, he saw a 54-car crash. Entering a bad old Utah fieldhouse one night, the players began to look for rats. "Back home," Elg said, "We had a rat so mean he had a name. We called him 'Timmy the rat.' Timmy would eat the food right off your plate. If you tried to swat him with a broom, Timmy would grab it right out of your hands and beat you with it."

I have a speaking voice that Hot Rod Hundley has described as pure hillbilly. It's not as bad as it used to be—not as southern as it used to be. Pete Newell, the Cal coach and our Olympic coach in 1960, just couldn't understand me when I spoke. Once he blew his stack. "For cryin' out loud, Jerry," he said, "speak English."

Elg doesn't seem to notice how much improved my speech is. "Rumors are safe with you, Tweety-bird," he says. "You pass 'em on, but no one can understand you." Elgin once said I sounded like I'd taken a course in public speaking—hog-calling."

Elg is the chief of everything and everyone. Once we had a vote on what color blazers to get. There was only one vote for blue. Elgin's vote. We got blue. Bill Russell admired us in our new blue blazers and said to Elg, "It was mighty democratic of you, Elg, to give the boys a vote."

"I gave 'em the vote. I didn't say I'd count 'em," Elg said.

On a flight once, LaRusso was idly flipping an old half-dollar. Elg wandered up and said, "If I call it, it's mine." Deuce knew it was hopeless. He shrugged and tossed the coin.

Elg called "heads." Deuce looked down at the coin and said, triumphantly, "I see an eagle. You lose, baby. Pay up."

Elg grabbed the coin and started to walk off. "Sorry friend," he said. "Eagles got heads, too."

In New York Elg and Tom Hawkins once were riding in a cab to the Garden. The cabbie asked, "You guys basketball players?" Elg said, "Naw, we're boxers. We're fighting the main tonight." He poked Hawk. "He," Elg said, "is gonna' lose to me tonight."

If they fought, Hawk would lose. There is no way to beat Elg at anything.

Chick Hearn has been driven practically out of his mind by his inability to beat Elg at cards. One night when he was getting murdered, Chick announced, "I think I've finally figured out a way to get even with you, old man."

Elg eyed him cynically. "What you gonna' do, Chickie-baby, pay me off in Chinese money?" he asked.

Without Elg where would I be? "Deuce" is gone from the team now. And "Stumpy." And "Darlin'." And "Astro-dome." And so many others. "Boomer" is gone from all of us. It's lonely without them.

We're men playing a boy's game. And we're boys playing a men's game. We're gypsies. Some of us come and go in the night. The best of us may not last 10 years. And not many seem to notice. And fewer remember. It's all exciting. And it pays well. But you get lonely, sometimes.

13
The Old Pro

I missed only one game during the 1965-66 regular-season schedule of 80 games. Bill Russell poked his finger in my eye during the All-Star game at mid-season and darn near blinded me. For a while the doctors were concerned about it, but the injury healed quickly and I only sat out one game. It was the last season I avoided serious injury. It's a lucky thing. Elgin missed 15 games and was below par in twice that many.

Baylor's broken kneecap had been repaired during the off-season in a delicate operation performed by Dr. Robert Kerlan, the Laker team physician. Recuperating, Elg had to endure a strenuous series of exercises. He sat out most of the first part of the season. When he did play, he held back for fear of re-injuring his knee. Then he twisted the other knee, the left knee, and was out three more weeks. I know he went through hell.

However, by the end of the season, he was beginning to play something like his old self again. If he is not quite the player he once was, few of us are. We all get older. All of us expected Elg to play again, but most of us did not expect him to play as well as he has. He has a lot of guts and determination.

Because of Baylor's injury, the Lakers traded guard Dick Barnett to New York for forward Bob Boozer. It was not a

Wilt led the overthrow of the Celtics in the 1966-67 season as
Philadelphia won the championship. MALCOLM W. EMMONS

good trade. Barnett helped us more with his coming off the bench and his shooting than Boozer did, because Boozer seems to be the kind of player who has to play regularly to be effective. The Lakers alternated him with LeRoy Ellis in Baylor's corner, opposite Rudy LaRusso, and Bob never seemed to settle down. Later, when he was sent to Chicago, he played regularly and played a lot better than he ever did with us. The Lakers also made a bad move when they let Don Nelson go to Boston. He had helped us and he went on to help Boston as a spot player. John Fairchild, a rookie forward whom we kept, never played much and was later dropped.

With Barnett gone, Walt Hazzard and Jim King alternated in the guard slot alongside me, with Gale Goodrich in reserve. Gale had carried on in Walt's shoes in leading UCLA to another NCAA championship. He's a hustler and very quick, but he's also only 6-1, which is very small for this league and a severe handicap. Still, we were all right in the backcourt. Hazzard had to learn to play in the pros. He had to learn to play defense, to make good plays, to get in a position for good shots. He's very flashy and sometimes too determined to do everything in a spectacular way. And he was unhappy at not having been given a regular role right away in pro ball. But he was very talented and as he moved up he began to show some of his talent. And the more Jim King played, the more he showed. He's quick and tough and a fair shooter.

Where we missed Elg most was not his shooting, but his rebounding. I averaged 31 points a game that season, second only to Wilt's 33. LaRusso, Ellis, Hazzard, and Boozer all averaged in double figures. We wound up scoring more points than we had the year before. But we couldn't control the ballgames the way a really outstanding pro team should because we couldn't get the ball enough. Darrall Imhoff, Gene Wiley, and LeRoy Ellis just weren't equal to beating Bill Russell, Wilt Chamberlain, Nate Thurmond, Walt Bellamy, Zelmo Beaty, and guys like that off the boards. The Lakers lacked that then. We couldn't fast-break like other teams because we couldn't count on our center pulling the ball down and throwing it downcourt to get things going. A small guard can't rebound much. It's not his job. When the situation presents itself, he can try to get good position, and if he has good anticipation and good timing, he'll pick off some. I get my share. Once I got 15 rebounds. I get more than some forwards. But Oscar Robertson gets more than I do. He's a better rebounder than I am, and the best rebounding guard I ever saw. Baylor is the best rebounding forward I ever saw. He has the strength, the timing, and the anticipation to move right in and take the ball away from some centers. Bob Pettit and Dolph Schayes were very good in their day, while Bailey Howell has been outstanding too.

When it counts, Bill Russell is the best rebounder of all. Wilt and Nate Thurmond are great rebounding centers, and John Kerr was very good when he played, but Russell is far and away the best the game has ever known. Actually, at 6-10 and 220 pounds, he's not the biggest center, but Bill seems to have a sixth sense as to where the ball will come off, he's a great leaper, he has powerful hands, he's unafraid, and he's absolutely determined to get the ball. He doesn't care about scoring. He'd rather get a rebound and let someone else shoot it up. Thurmond is quite a bit like him. If he can avoid serious injuries, which he has not in recent years, he can be the best after Russell retires, which has to happen some day.

Although this is a game of possession, the Lakers won without good rebounding because we hustled and we always were a good shooting club. We ran a lot and got good penetration. In other words, we work our way through the other team's defenses. But we were never physically equipped to overpower anyone, dominate the backboards and the games, win easily. We always had to work harder than most clubs to win.

Despite Elgin's troubled season, we put together a 45-35 record and won the West by seven games over Baltimore during 1965-66. Baltimore dealt Bellamy to New York, but good seasons from Howell, Ohl, Gus Johnson, and Kevin Loughery made them tough. St. Louis added Joe Caldwell and Rod Thorn, who had followed Rod Hundley and me to All-American honors at West Virginia, but badly missed Bob Pettit, who had been the guts of that ball club and who had retired. The Hawks finished third. San Francisco, with Rick Barry, a hot rookie who averaged 25 a game, finished fourth. Detroit, with Terry Dischinger in the service, finished fifth.

Personally, I had my moments. Early that December I scored 51 against Cincinnati in Los Angeles. Exactly one week later I scored 51 again, this time in Cincinnati. I guess Oscar brings out the best in me. I scored 46 against Boston in L.A. in one game and 46 in New York in another game. All told, I scored 40 or more points ten times, then twice more in the playoffs. In a game against San Francisco I set a personal record by hitting 20 of 21 free throws. I also hit 20 in two other games and 19 in two games. I finished second to Wilt in the MVP voting.

The big upheaval came in the East, and Wilt played a big part in it. Philadelphia added a good rookie, Billy Cunningham, to its powerful forecourt of Wilt, Luke Jackson, and Chet Walker, and another fine rookie, Wally Jones, to go with the gifted Greer in the backcourt. Boston missed Tom Heinsohn, who had retired. Philly took Boston to the wire, then beat them out by one game. Cincinnati, standing pat, faded to third. Meanwhile, New York, adding Bellamy and Barnett, was building up.

Everyone figured Boston was aging and fading fast. Everyone was wrong, as everyone often is. The Celtics simply lost a tough pennant race to a tough club. They had won nine straight pennants and losing one shook them. In the opening round of their playoff series against Cincy, the Celts lost two of the first three, both at home. But they bounced back to win the next two and the series. And then they took Philly apart four games out of five to advance to the finals once again.

Meanwhile, St. Louis swept Baltimore three straight, then took us on. The Hawks always seemed to be strong physically. Over the years I've played in the NBA, the Hawks have been the roughest team we've played. It's all right. That's the way the game is played these days. The Hawks do it very well. They gave us a good going over in that series. On one play, Zelmo Beaty knocked me ten feet. I landed with a thud, aching in every bone. Before the series was over, I twisted my right instep, jammed the ring finger on my shooting hand and the thumb on my left hand.

We won the first two and three of the first four, but the Hawks wouldn't stay down. They won two straight to tie the series before we won the deciding game in L.A., 130-121. I had five fouls at the end of three quarters, but had learned to play with fouls by then. On defense I used my body more than my hands. On offense I laid off the drive. I never got the sixth foul, didn't foul out, and had a big last period as we put them away. But one close call and that might have been it.

Now we had another crack against Boston in the playoff finals. Just like old times. They still had the odd-game edge and the advantage of opening the series with two games at home. We shook them up in the opener. They got us 18 points down and thought we were broken. We got hot and wound up winning, 133-129, in overtime. I got 41, Baylor 36, Goodrich 20. I got nine in the overtime. Boston came roaring back to win the second, 129-109. I was bad, scoring just 18. We lost by 20, but many nights I might score 20 more. You see how easy it is to blame yourself.

In Los Angeles, they took us two straight, 120-106 and 122-117. I got 34 in the first and 45 in the second. We did not play well. We just couldn't seem to get untracked. We figured they were better than us, but we also figured we might upset them. Now, suddenly, we were down three games to one. We had looked so bad we were embarrassed. Were they that much better? Everyone figured we were dead. Again, everyone was wrong. Or almost wrong.

In the fifth game at Boston, Baylor bounced back, netting 41. I got 31, 14 in the last quarter. We were even with 35 seconds to play. I hit a jumper. They brought the ball down, but we got it back. I drove and was fouled. I hit both free throws with eight seconds left. We won, 121-117. So we went back to Los Angeles. I got 32, Goodrich 28, LaRusso 20. It was a big team effort before 15,000 and we won, 123-115.

Now the series was even. No team ever had come from 1-3 to win the best-of-seven NBA final. Presumably we now had the momentum. Momentum is nice, but it's overrated. Momentum can change hands swiftly in sports. In pro basketball, a team has a hot streak and gains momentum. Then the other team streaks back. Usually each team has a hot streak each game. Very often the team that has a second hot streak wins.

We barreled back into old Boston Garden before a capacity crowd screaming for our blood. We had the momentum. They had Russell. He got 25 points and 32 rebounds. If I haven't mentioned him throughout this series, it's because he's taken for granted. He's always there, doing what he does. I scored 36. They streaked at the start and pulled away. We couldn't put anything together.

They had us, 95-85, in the last few minutes. That was awful. In this high-scoring game, especially in a championship game, that was really awful. We got a basket. Another. Another. Another. Suddenly it was 95-93 and the place was going crazy. But it was too late. The buzzer sounded. That buzzer. And the Celtics went into their victory dance.

Red Auerbach puffed on his cigar. Eight straight NBA titles and this was his last as coach. He was retiring from the bench to the front office, to be replaced by player-coach Bill

Russell. If we were ever going to beat them, we were not now ever going to beat them with Auerbach. He had beaten us many times, and now he had beaten us forever.

During the summer the bosses tore up our team and in the 1966-67 season we slipped badly.

Chicago came back into the league with a new franchise, restoring the league to balance with ten teams. In the expansion draft, we let Bob Boozer and Jim King go. We kept players, some kids, who were not as good or experienced as Boozer and King. We missed them badly. We traded LeRoy Ellis to Baltimore for Jim Barnes. Ellis was a part of our team, more versatile and more consistent than Barnes. We missed Ellis badly. During the season, we traded Rudy LaRusso and obtained Mel Counts. Rudy was an exceptional passer for a big foward, he did lot of things well and he complemented Elgin in the front court perfectly. He may not have liked a subordinate role, but he handled it very well. Counts was a seven-footer, but green. Some day he may be very good, better than LaRusso, but he was not that then. We also dropped Gene Wiley. We added two fine rookies, Archie Clark and Jerry Chambers, and regained Tom Hawkins, but we lost more than we gained.

For me, personally, it was a dreadful season. I averaged more than 28 points a game, but played only 66 out of the 81 games scheduled during the regular season. I was ready to go until I injured my foot in the last game of the exhibition campaign. I missed the first nine games, then took 16 more games to get back in shape. I think I hurt the club because I had to play myself back into shape. We suffered early losses which affected our whole season. If our attitude had been better, we wouldn't have lost some of the games we lost that season. I suffered from nagging injuries all season.

There were a few good moments, personally. I got 45 against Baltimore and 44 against San Francisco. I got 23 free throws in one game against Philadelphia. I hit 16 for 16 in a game against San Francisco. I got 16 in the All-Star game as the West, coached by Schaus, beat the East, coached by Auerbach, 135-120, at San Francisco. The real stars were San Francisco's Rick Barry, who scored 38, and Nate Thurmond, who got 16 points and 18 rebounds. Barry got 50 or more points in five games that season and led the league with an average of 35 a game.

Barry and Thurmond led San Francisco to the Western pennant by five games over St. Louis, which had added a fine rookie, Lou Hudson. We finished three games further back at 36-45, the worst single record I've ever had in pro ball. The new Chicago team finished fourth, beating out Detroit, though Detroit came up with an outstanding rookie in Dave Bing.

In the East, Philadelphia, with Chamberlain feeding off and playing defense and averaging only 24 points, beat out Boston for the divisional title by eight games. Chamberlain was supported by Jackson, Walker, Cunningham, and Greer. Boston had added Bailey Howell and Wayne Embry, but missed Auerbach on the bench. It is very hard for a man to play and coach at the same time, as Bill Russell had to, and the Celtics had to adjust.

Baltimore fell into last place. New York added Cazzie Russell, who was not ready yet, and finished fourth. Jack Twyman had retired and Cincinnati finished third.

In the Eastern playoff finals, Philadelphia eliminated Boston, four games to one, and was ready for the Western division champion. Philadelphia was very powerful and the Celtics were in a time of transition and just had a real bad series. It was about time, I guess.

In the first minute of our first playoff game, against San Francisco, I broke my right hand. I did not play another minute. The playoffs did not last many minutes for our team. San Francisco swept us three straight, a humiliating experience. St. Louis took Chicago, but was eliminated by San Francisco in the Western finals. Then San Francisco fell to Philadelphia in six games for the championship.

After eight straight titles, the Celtics were just another bunch of losers, like us.

Coach van Breda Kolff is a tough ex-Marine who squirms, twists, jumps and stomps. MALCOLM W. EMMONS

14
New Coach

The 1967-68 season was one of great change. First, we got a new manager and a new coach. Our general manager, Lou Mohs, died. He had been aging and ailing, but still it was a shock. He was a fine person. Fred Schaus moved upstairs to take his place. Mr. Cooke brought in Bill van Breda Kolff from Princeton as the new coach. At mid-season we moved into the new Forum in the Los Angeles suburb in Inglewood. Most of all, I felt as though I'd joined the Marines that season. Actually, the Marines joined us.

Van Breda Kolff is an ex-Marine, very tough.

He came out of the Ivy League, but if we expected a polite guy, a rah-rah type, we were wrong. He doesn't fool around. He says what he thinks. But you can see he's just being honest. He doesn't play favorites. All the players are alike to him. He doesn't run around buttering up the stars. I don't think he had a flattering word to say to me or about me all season. But he just wants to win, which we all do. We could see that. He can call you a son of a something or threaten to punch you in the nose, but it doesn't make you hate him, it just makes you want to do better to show him you can do what he seems to think you can't do. He's very inspiring that way. It's his personality. It's a chemistry. Some guys have it and some don't.

This is a game of emotion and van Breda Kolff is much more emotional than Schaus was.

Coaches don't give pep talks any more. Not many, anyway. They don't work. Ball players are too sophisticated. But Bill comes close. He's always talking. He's a big talker. And he's always building up. He tells us what he expects us to find out there and what he expects us to do. If we're playing Boston or Philly, clubs with big centers, he stresses that we'll have to help out on the boards, run a lot, play for real good shots. If we're playing Cincinnati, he may tell me to take Robertson until he gets me in foul trouble. He's always needling. If we're playing a weak club, maybe a new club like Seattle, he reminds us he doesn't want us to give the game away like the last time we played them. He builds and builds. "All right, here we go," he says, clapping his hands together, and we run out to slay the dragon, hollering so the dragon knows we're coming and can run away if he wants.

During games, Bill's very excitable. He won't last long at this rate. He squirms and twists and jumps and stomps. He hates rough play. He's always on the refs: "Holy gee whiz, Jim, are you gonna' let that man get away with that . . . Hey, Manny, give him an ax and let's be done with it . . . Aw, come on, Sid, that was terrible . . . terrible . . . TERRIBLE!" He got socked with about 60 technical fouls and a few fines his first two seasons and got kicked out of a few games. The refs can get back at him. We can't. He's always on us, yelling from the bench or during time outs: "Hey, Jerry, is he your man or does he have special privileges? . . . Hey, Mel, how about blocking out on those rebounds? Have I been talking to myself all this time? . . . You guys been in this league eight, ten years and you act like high school kids. I had freshmen at Princeton from Punxatawnie, Pennsylvania, knew more basketball than you clowns." He doesn't even stop after the games are over. After one game he chased Elg clear back to the dressing room, screaming, "Ten years an all-pro and you make a mistake a grade-school kid wouldn't make."

Elgin took it. I took it. We all did, because he showed us something. He reminded us no matter how many years we played in this game, we still have things to learn and we still can improve. He reminded us that there's different ways to play this game. He showed us he really knows the game, which we respect. He showed us he loses hard, which we respect. He showed us he plays fair, which we respect. He showed he's the boss on court, which we respect.

Schaus and I had been coach and player together for 10 seasons, since my first varsity season in college. A lot of people wondered how I'd be affected by the change. It did affect me. After all these years, Fred and I understood each other. We didn't have to talk over a lot of things, which were just understood. Van Breda Kolff and I very quickly came to understand each other even better. When he came under great pressure from Wilt and the press in his second season, and really stood up to it with dignity, I came to admire him even more. "Butch" is quite a guy and I've never enjoyed anything much more than playing under him.

In some ways the change helped me, and helped us. Fred had been coaching the club and a lot of the guys a long time. He was close to us and we liked him and he liked us and he may have gotten a little soft on us. He had nothing new to say to guys like Elg and me. He didn't give us orders, he made suggestions. Van Breda Kolff wasn't awed by us. He brought us new things and he put it to us and no backtalk. He challenged us to please him, which made all of us pick up the pace.

At first I could see van Breda Kolff was disappointed in me. He'd heard a lot about me and he felt I wasn't showing him much. But I was injured and hurting. Around mid-season, when I began to feel better, I began to play better. To be honest, I think I played the best all-around ball of my career the last third of the season. I could see van Breda Kolff felt better about me. And I felt good about that.

By not trying to be one of the guys, he became one. He really loves the game and the guys. He said once, "All I care about is my family and the guys. You play the game, you have a few beers, you go home, and that's it, that's life."

Basketball is Schaus's life, too. He was a fine coach and he should be a very good general manager. His strength has always been that he knows the game as well as anyone ever knew it and was always willing to work hard at it and could get the guys under him to work hard at it. He was a great organizer and he ran excellent practices. His teams were always well conditioned and never seemed to run into problems with games they hadn't prepared for in practice.

Schaus had been in the big-time awhile. He knew the pro life. Van Breda Kolff is just finding out what it is. The traveling, the tough schedule, the rough play tore him apart his first season. He showed us he has a lot to learn. But if he survives, he should be a good one.

He's one of the few coaches brought up from the college game to the pro game in recent years. A lot of people wonder why the experienced, successful college coaches aren't brought into the NBA more. A lot of people wonder why pro clubs prefer to elevate ex-pros, some of whom were just ordinary players and aren't big names. There are good reasons.

The college game is entirely different from the pro game. The college coach has to spend a lot of time recruiting talent. When he gets the players, he has to do a lot of teaching. And he keeps trying to make men out of kids. He has to keep them eligible. He has to mother them. He sees that everyone has a seat on the bench and a towel. He disciplines them: "Don't get a drink of water when I'm talking to you, son," he says. If he's got one outstanding ball player and if he gets the rest of the guys to pull together, he's got a winner. He only has to hold it over 25 or 30 games and he doesn't have much traveling to worry about. By comparison his life is soft.

The pro coach has a tough life. He's always traveling with his club, playing 100 games or so a season. He doesn't have time to practice his players much or teach much. By the time he gets them, they're pretty well grooved anyway. In the pro game, he's stuck with the talent he has or the talent the front office will go out and get for him. It doesn't matter if he was a great player or has a great mind, there's only so much he can do with what he has. This isn't football. He can't benefit from hours of studying films, diagraming plays, planning strategies. He can work like hell and it won't get him a darn thing.

There's only so much any coach can bring to a team and a game. No coach is a miracle man. None I ever saw, anyway. He either has a super-star or two or he doesn't. One or two men make the difference. With Bill Russell, Red Auerbach always finished first. Without him, he doesn't. I don't think there are many college coaches around who could do better than the pro coaches we have. The college coaches don't know the pro game and the problems of the pro players the way the pro coaches and the ex-pro players do. They don't fit in as well.

I am absolutely convinced that the most important thing any coach on any level can have is a winning personality. It's more important in pro ball than anywhere else, because the guys are harder to sell. They're grown men with families, playing for pay. If they respect the coach, he'll get the most out of them. If not, he'll waste what he's got.

In my time in the NBA, three or four coaches have stood out in my mind aside from Schaus. First on my list would be Alex Hannum. I always wanted to play for Alex. I really think he gets his teams ready to play. They're always enthusiastic, always good mechanically, always interesting to watch. He knows basketball, he knows the pro game, and he's a beautiful personality who inspires the guys to do a job. He brought out the best in Wilt. He brought out the best in a lot of guys.

Next on the list would be Red Auerbach. Frankly, I don't think he's as sharp technically as some. Maybe he is but I don't think it's very important. He had a feel for the tempo of a game and was the best I've observed at making substitutions, which is an art in itself. He knows when a man should come out and when a man should go in. He makes everyone feel a part of the team. He knows what's needed to change a game. And his teams always hustled and were always alert to take advantage of mistakes.

Then come Bill Sharman and Richie Guerin. Both are young as pro coaches go, but both are blessed with the sort of personalities that make pro coaches good. Guerin has a very fiery personality. His clubs work hard, play tough, move the ball well, and don't make many mistakes. Sharman is calmer, but the guys really want to play for him. He conditions his team well and manipulates his talent well.

The San Francisco team of 1967-68 was not as good as Sharman made it seem to be. The league lost a lot when Sharman jumped to the Los Angeles team of the ABA.

Generally, I think the importance of coaches in basketball is overrated. They're at the mercy of their talent. There's not much to choose among most of them. But there are five or six who do a little more of what can be done.

Van Breda Kolff came in determined to make the Lakers play more team ball. He could see the Lakers leaned heavily on Baylor and me and he wanted to spread things around more. Up to a point that's a laudable ambition. But you can't win if everyone shoots the same number of times. If you're going to win, your best shooters have to take the most shots. In the end, the Lakers wound up leaning on Baylor and me just like always.

If I thought that 1966-67 had been bad for me as far as injuries were concerned, I was really just finding out what a bad injury season could be. I was injured on and off the entire 1967-68 season. In an exhibition game in October, San Francisco's Fred Hetzel kneed me in the thigh. In another exhibition that month, Baltimore's Gus Johnson hit me in the face with a karate chop. Along the way, I jammed my left hand. I played with it, but when it got sore and swollen, I had it X-rayed just before the start of the regular season. It turned out I had broken a bone. The hand had to be put in a cast and I missed the first 12 games.

After I got back in action, Johnny Green of San Diego rammed me on a rebound and I came down on my hip, bruising it badly. I missed a couple of games. I was just rounding into shape when Connie Dierking of Cincinnati caught me in the face with a forearm, breaking my nose again. I missed a couple more games. Later in the season, Walt Bellamy of New York got his elbow in my face and broke my nose once again. Then I pulled a groin muscle, which is really a painful injury, and sat out the last part of the season. I missed 31 of our 82 regular-season games. Then I hurt my foot in the playoffs and limped the rest of the way.

Still, it was a surprising season for us.

San Diego and Seattle joined the league with new franchises bringing the NBA up to 12 teams. We let John Block and Henry Finkel, two big reserve forwards, go to San Diego, and we let Hazzard go to Seattle in the expansion draft. Walter was just becoming a pretty good ball player. At Seattle he got to play regularly and averaged 24 points a game. We could have used him, especially when I was hurt so much. Still, we had a good year. Baylor had a fine season, averaging 26 points a game, second best in the league. I averaged 26 points in the games I played. Archie Clark really developed, averaging almost 20. Goodrich began to overcome his lack of height. Imhoff, improving with age, played pretty good cen-

194

ter, despite a bad back, and Counts backed him up well.
Hawkins gave us a lot of zip up front. Defensively this was
the best team I've ever played with.

My injuries handicapped the team a lot in the first half
of the season, but from mid-season on, we came on like
gang-busters. From mid-season on, I think we were the best
team in the NBA.

In his second full season as coach of St. Louis, Guerin
really got the Hawks rolling. Lou Hudson spent most of the
season in the Army, but the Hawks played aggressively and
got off to a tremendous start, which sustained them all year.
In San Francisco, Rick Barry jumped to the ABA, then was
sidelined by a lawsuit, and Nate Thurmond got hurt, but the
Warriors acquired LaRusso, and Sharman got tremendous mile-
age out of what he had.

We were third most of the season, but passed San Francisco
and moved to within four games of the Hawks at the finish.
We were 52-30 and they were 56-26 at the end. Now we
had a chance in the playoffs to show how much we had
improved. Throw out the regular season. It's unfair, but that's
the way it is.

We opened at home with two against Chicago. We won
both, coasting, 109-101 and 111-106. In the third game, in
Chicago, Flynn Robinson, a talented shooter who can get
hot, got hot and scored 41 and sank us, 104-98. In the next
game, van Breda Kolff assigned me to him. He got four baskets.
I limited him, but I had to work so hard at it that it took
away my offense. I hit only five of 19 shots. But we did win,
93-87, so it worked. Back in L.A., we wrapped it up, 122-99.

San Francisco upset St. Louis, four games to two, knocking
the regular-season champion out of the playoffs. Now we had
a chance to atone for the previous season's three straight
playoff losses to San Francisco. We got it, winning four
straight. In one, I hit 14 of 20 shots from the field and
totaled 40 points. We took the final one, 106-100, in San
Francisco. At that point, we'd never been hotter.

In the East, Hannum's powerful Philadelphia team, with Wilt averaging just 24 points a game and playing the whole game again, went 62-20 and beat out Boston by eight games to win its third straight pennant. Boston missed K. C. Jones, who had retired. New York, adding Bill Bradley, who wasn't ready, and Walt Frazier, continued on the rise to third place. Detroit, in this division now, finished fourth, although Bing took the scoring title with a 27-point average. Cincy sank into the cellar.

In the playoffs, Philly took New York, four games to two, while Boston beat Detroit, four games to two. Then Boston, inspired by Russell, won a seesaw series from Philadelphia, four games to three. They won the first one, lost three straight, then came back brilliantly to win three straight and the series. It was sensational. But it figured to exhaust them.

We were better rested, younger, hungrier, hotter. This was not the best Laker team I'd played on, but expansion had diluted the strength of the best teams. For the first time, I really felt we were as good as any team in the league. Maybe Philly was better but they were out of it. If we ever had a chance to beat Boston, this seemed to be it. If we ever should have been favored over Boston, this was the time. I was very hopeful going in.

We went into the first one at Boston really rolling. We got them down by 15. Maybe that was the worst thing that ever happened to us. It was just the start of the series, but we began to play like we could coast in. Russell began to sweep the boards and they began to hit and they passed us and won, 107-101. Angrily, we bounced back to take the second one, 123-113. I got 35 and felt better.

Now we had them in L.A. A crowd of 17,011 packed the Forum. I got 33, but we blew it, 127-119. A bigger crowd, 17,147, turned out two nights later and we evened the series, 118-105. All season van Breda Kolff had been getting fined and kicked out of games for protests that brought him technical fouls. He did it in this one and Goodrich coached

I'm driving well against Boston's John Havlicek, but in the fifth game of the playoffs I collided with John and badly sprained my ankle. LOS ANGELES LAKERS

to the end. Gale forgot to take me out after the issue was settled.

In the waning moments of the game, I collided with Havlicek as we went after a loose ball out of bounds. I had no business diving after loose balls at that point. The game was decided. But if you're playing, how can you not go after loose balls? Should I have just stood there and let Havlicek have the ball? Maybe I should have just sat down on the court and waited for the buzzer.

I went down heavily and sprained my left ankle severely. I lay there a moment, cursing. I limped to the dressing room. The doc looked it over and said he thought it might be OK. Schaus and van Breda Kolff told the writers they thought it would be OK. I said I'd play. I was angry and determined. But my ankle was badly sprained. I received treatment and did play from then on, but awkwardly. Actually, though no one knew it, the groin hurt more than the foot.

Back in Boston for the fifth game, we trailed by 19 points. But we kept pounding at them. We crept closer and closer. Near the end, we blew some easy baskets that would have won it. With 12 seconds left, I drove in and got a lay-up to tie it. They lost the ball and we got a chance to win it. Taking the ball out of bounds, the pass went to Baylor. Off balance, running out of time, he had to shoot. He hit iron and the ball bounced away.

We went into overtime. They got ahead, but we hung on. I hit a jumper to tie it at 117-all with less than one minute to play. The noise in that gloomy old building pounded at me. Havlicek threw in a 20-foot jumper to put Boston ahead by two. But we had time to tie it. I wanted the shot. But in the huddle van Breda Kolff said to play the pass to anyone who was free. The toss went to Elg. Nelson was guarding him. Baylor yo-yoed his dribble, suddenly spun and shot. From nowhere, Russell slapped the shot away. I managed to get 38 points, but they won, 120-117.

In Los Angeles, 17,392 came to see the sixth and, as it turned out, the final game. The Celtics shot 50 percent as a team. Havlicek got 40, Howell 30. Russell got all the rebounds. They won, 124-109. It wasn't even close.

The same old story. Boston. I had been in the league eight seasons. We had reached the finals and lost to Boston five times. We walked down to our dressing room, which was closed to the writers and outsiders for a while. We sat there sweaty and sore and sick of losing, without speaking for a long time. Then someone said, "When do we get our playoff checks?" I couldn't believe it. I looked at him angrily. How could a player think of money at a time like this? We all want our money, but not then, not when we'd just lost what we've never won and might have won. You just can't say this game and winning mean the same to all players. You just can't say it. I don't think any team ever had better spirit or wanted to win much more than the Laker teams I've played on, but not everyone had it, not everyone.

I sat there remembering twice this game when the ball was on the floor and Siegfried dove for it. He didn't just go for it hard—he dove for it. And they're all that way on the Celtics. You can't teach it. Everyone wants to win. It's more fun and pays better. But the willingness to do anything you have to do to win, the willingness to spill your guts, the willingness to sacrifice yourself—this you can't teach and you can't talk into a man. What really hurt me then was that I felt we had thrown away two games in this series—the first game and the fifth game—and we had lost it at home. We could have won it. We really could have won it. Maybe not too many of the others, but this one.

Slowly, I stripped off my sweaty uniform and dropped it on the rug and walked off to the shower. I stood under the hot water trying to steam the soreness out of my body. Van Breda Kolff had been holding the press at bay outside the dressing room door, telling them why we'd lost, but now they were inside, asking us. I have no complaints with writers. I've been very lucky. I've had a fine career and have been involved in very little controversy and no scandal. I've had

When it comes to winning, there is no one like Bill Russell.
MALCOLM W. EMMONS

mostly fine things written about me—a lot of praise and very little criticism. Sometimes you're misquoted. Sometimes there are inaccuracies. Sometimes you can see the writers don't all know the game too well. But I have no real complaints.

I'm not the best copy. What I do on the court is fine, but I don't do much off court. I don't sit around belting a few down and passing small talk with the writers, which they like, understandably, and which makes them feel close to the ball players and gives them a chance to hear things said that a ball player ordinarily might not say. I've said some things here I want to say, but ordinarily I don't want to talk a whole lot. I don't want to knock players or get involved in guessing games as to why things happened. If we've won, I'll try to spread the credit around. Lord knows I get too much, and a lot of good, unselfish guys don't get enough. If we've lost, I'm usually so disappointed I don't want to talk about it. I hurt inside, real bad. A writer comes up and asks me why and I say, "I don't know. Please ask someone else." I try to be polite. I know he's got a job to do, but someone else will have to help him. I'm sorry, but I'm just no good in these situations.

I did talk, though, when Bill Russell came out of the Celtic dressing room and began to walk through the crowd and some writer asked me about him. Russell, bearded, wearing a frock coat, stately, and smiling. They can talk about individual players in any sport, I said, but when it comes to winning, there is no one like him. I know some of those guys in other sports, in baseball and football, are great, but I don't think there's ever been anyone to compare to him. What has he won then? Ten championships. Ten championships in 12 years. I play this game and I know. I've been through all the trying and the rough stuff and the broken bones and the broken noses and the pulled muscles and the sprained ankles and the big shots that went in and the big shots that didn't go in and I know.

15
A Time To Cry

One of the most dramatic deals in basketball history brought us Wilt Chamberlain before the 1968-69 season began. To get Wilt, Mr. Cooke parted with Darrall Imhoff, Archie Clark, Jerry Chambers and cash. Reportedly, he also had to guarantee Wilt a $250,000 annual salary on a five-year contract. Frankly, I know no more about this than I read in the papers, but I suspect it's pretty close to accurate. Possibly Mr. Cooke felt increased attendance would return his investment. Possibly he wanted an NBA title so much he was willing to buy one if it was possible. I don't think it's possible.

The NBA is a tough league which gets tougher every year. With the addition of Phoenix and Milwaukee for the 1968-69 season, it had grown to 14 teams. Further expansion seems inevitable. If the American Basketball Association does not make it, some of its cities may be added. The Hawks were shifted from St. Louis into Atlanta. Further shifts are always possible. Things are always changing. It's hard to settle down. And it's hard to win.

It's true that expansion has diluted the talent some. However, more good talent is available than ever before. More boys are playing basketball than ever before. With NBA expansion, there is more incentive for more boys to work for pro careers. If the ABA survives, there would be more room yet. Which is why I, like most basketball players, root sym-

On good nights Wilt can beat some teams all by himself and he may be the first player ever to do this. MALCOLM W. EMMONS

pathetically for the new league. Which does not mean I would jump to it. Never. Like others, I was approached to see if I was interested. I told them at this point in my career, I would hardly consider leaving the Lakers.

Some of the players on expansion teams are ridiculed. Perhaps there are players in this league who wouldn't have made it some years ago. On the other hand, many of these are better than many who made it in those years. Just look at the shooting percentages. And while there's no statistical way to measure defense, the players of today are bigger, faster and better-schooled, so I suspect they're superior in most departments.

In its second season, San Diego came up with a fine, strong, high-scoring front man in Elvin Hayes, leading a big front line that was able to give everyone trouble. We let Gale Goodrich go to Phoenix in the expansion draft. Given the room to stretch out, little "Stumpy" had a great season and proved he could play with the big boys. Seattle traded Walt Hazzard to the Hawks for Len Wilkens, and Len and Bob Rule made the Sonics tough. The Hawks and Warriors remained tough. The West was no snap.

The Eastern Division was tougher. Boston was aging, but could not be counted out. New York traded Walt Bellamy to Detroit for Dave DeBusschere and improved itself. With Willis Reed playing center and a clever and fast-improving Walt Frazier sparking the backcourt, the Knicks began to get very good. Despite the loss of Chamberlain, Philadelphia was still strong and Imhoff and Clark fit in very well. And with a powerful and unselfish rookie, Wes Unseld, added to Earl Monroe and Gus Johnson, Baltimore had its best team ever.

Milwaukee was an also-ran in this company, but, getting Lew Alcindor, they will be great in the future. Lew is a big man who can shoot. If he is rugged and determined enough, he can be one of the great ones. With Pete Maravich, Rick Mount and Spencer Haywood coming up, among others, there is no shortage of talent available to the NBA.

Most persons felt that all we had needed was a great center and that with Wilt we could not lose. And we didn't lose much. However, there is more to winning basketball than one great player, or even two or three. To get Wilt, we had to strip ourselves of some of our depth. We acquired Keith Erickson and Johnny Egan to go with Freddie Crawford opposite me at guard. And we added a promising rookie, Bill Hewitt, to go with Mel Counts opposite Elgin at forward. It was practically a brand-new team and a fairly thin one.

It was nonsense to say, as many did, that we'd need three basketballs after Wilt joined us. We managed with one all these years, and we were sure willing to give Wilt a piece of it if he'd help us win. However, it's not that easy. We each have our distinctive styles. It was our job as pros to adjust these styles so we could do our best individually and our best together. It was a challenge to van Breda Kolff, who does not go in as much as many coaches do for intense practices, special plans for each team, and set plays.

Actually, I don't think we had the best team in 1968-69 Wilt has ever played on. Teams that have deliberate players and a lot of good outside shooters suit him better than our team did. Philadelphia with Chet Walker, Billy Cunningham and Luke Jackson in the corners, and Hal Greer and Wally Jones in the backcourt had more good men to complement him than the Lakers had. We had still not settled on a starting lineup eight months after the season began, when the playoffs and the season ended.

No player is perfect. Chamberlain has his weaknesses. But he also has great strengths. He is the biggest and strongest man ever to play this game. He is limited to his fadeaway and dunk, but when he goes hard for the basket and the board, he is almost impossible to stop. He has scored more points and taken down more rebounds than any player in history. He destroys ordinary foes. On inspired nights, he can beat some teams all by himself. He is one of the few players who could ever do this.

Wilt refuses rest and plays just about every minute of every game. He is almost always there. With Wilt clogging up the middle, we could gamble more on defense, knowing Wilt would be backing us up, intimidating anyone who broke in, and blocking shots. This was especially valuable to a gambling defender like me. With Wilt rebounding, Elg didn't have to hit the boards as hard as he used to and we were seldom dominated on the boards. With Wilt getting us the ball, many times we got second and third shots we never had before. When Wilt would rebound defensively and feed off fast, we could really run on fast breaks.

However, he is not as flexible as he might be. He prefers playing in a low position, which often blocks off the middle for drives. He doesn't get the ball out well on fast breaks, or move out to set many screens for our outside shots. There is a tendency to play off Wilt, to just get the ball to him and let him make the plays, which slowed us to a walk and caused us to stand around sometimes, though we didn't have the personnel to run a lot anyway. And foes could afford to foul him freely. We wouldn't have lost many games if he could have hit just a fair share of free throws. But he wasn't the only poor free-throw shooter on the team. We had more than our share.

I think the key to Wilt is that he never has decided how he should play. Early in his career, he may have shot too much. Now, he may not shoot enough. His style varies from game to game. Unlike Russell, Wilt never settled into a groove. However, unlike Russell, Wilt bounced from team to team and his teams always wanted different things of him, while Russell could remain a defensive specialist who was never called on to produce points. With the Lakers, van Breda Kolff wanted Wilt to move around more. They even disagreed on whether he should rest Wilt from time to time. Wilt prefers to stay in, and in place, and he is used to getting his way.

I think Wilt has been more versatile and a greater player than Russell, but I think Russell has been a more valuable player because he is more settled-down, is better able to fit in with a team, and most important, can rise to the heights far better when it is needed. For one series or one game, Russell is superior, and in pro basketball the final laurels of each season usually rest on what happens in one last series or even just one last game.

When Wilt joined us, we had to learn to live together off the court as well as learn to play together on the court. They say Wilt is tough to live with. He is. He has great highs and lows and no in-betweens, and he is bluntly outspoken.

I feel that Elg and I have had a very special relationship all these years. I don't think there's ever been anything quite like it in our game. We've shared responsibility and laurels, times of jubilation and times of depression, and if we're cut from different cloth, if we're not close personal friends, we have never spoken a single cross word to one another, nor even been imagined in any kind of a disagreement. It would not be possible to admire anyone more than I admire Elg. He acts very cool about things, yet I've never known a great star who worked as hard as he worked, nor anyone who came back from a more difficult injury problem. He is a remarkable person.

When Wilt joined the Lakers, he, Elg, and I had passed 30, had been in the league nine or ten years, were set in our ways and fixed in our opinions, were breaking in with a brand new bunch of players, and yet were under the pressure of being expected to produce miracles. It was an uneasy situation.

In the first part of the season, Wilt's differences of opinion with van Breda Kolff created a strained atmosphere in the locker room and on the court. The press was aware of the trouble, which Wilt never tried to hide, and the writers wrote about it, which added to the pressure. For the first time since I'd been with the Lakers, we did not have a happy team.

However, as the season wore along, Wilt and Bill found a way to live together. Wilt began to get along with the other players better, we were winning, and the strain eased considerably. There was still some strain because the writers seemed unaware of this truce and the change that gradually came over us, and they continued to write of the original disagreements, scratching old sores. Everyone, including the writers, always seems to be on Wilt's back. Everyone knows about how much money he's making and expects him to be a superman, which he's not. All of this must contribute to his moodiness.

In his long career, Wilt has won only one championship. But Elg and I have never won even one. No man can win a championship alone. The fact is that this year we didn't have quality balance or depth, or experience playing together. Yet, while we didn't always look good, we did have games in which we were great, and we won and kept on winning until we had won the most games any Laker team ever won—55 games on a long 82-game schedule. Because of Wilt, we were even better defensively than the year before. These things didn't seem to matter to the press. I guess they figured we should go unbeaten.

It was a difficult season for me personally again as I had to deal with injuries all season again. I had two consecutive pulled hamstring muscles, a pulled thigh muscle, a pulled groin muscle, a charley horse and I was even out one time with the flu. I missed 21 games and there were times when I was disgusted and discouraged again.

However, I did have my nights. One night I hit 39, another time 44 when I hit 15 out of 20 from the field and 14 straight from the foul line. I wound up leading the Lakers in scoring average with just under 26 points a game and assists with more than 400. I had to handle the ball more than in recent years.

Wilt averaged 20 points and more than 20 rebounds a game and led the league in rebounding and shooting percentage. He had 66 points in one game against Phoenix and 42 rebounds in one game against Boston. Elg also had a fine season, averaging just under 25 points a game. We stayed in front all season and wound up winning the division over Atlanta by seven games, with San Francisco third, San Diego fourth, and Chicago, Seattle and Phoenix missing the playoffs.

Through injuries, Baltimore lost Gus Johnson, Philadelphia lost Luke Jackson and New York lost Cazzie Russell, but they staged a great race in the Eastern Division with the Bullets winning out by two games over Philly and three over the Knicks. Boston had a lot of injuries and seemed lethargic at times and fell to fourth, far off the pace. But they made the playoffs and that's what counts, because it's a new season in the playoffs whether that's right or wrong. Cincinnati, Detroit and Milwaukee missed the playoffs.

Although we had won only three games more than the previous season, I did feel we had a better chance of winning the playoffs than ever before. I thought we might not have to face Boston again. If we did we had Wilt to match Russell now and we had a season under our belt learning to play together with our new cast. I was healthy going in, as was Elg, who had been given a big night in his honor late in the season. It seemed like just maybe this might be our year at last. I couldn't help hoping.

I know our fans were hoping, too. We'd drawn a record 465,695 for an average of more than 11,000 fans for each of our 41 home games during the regular season, and we were to draw another record 160,958 more for an average of more than 16,000 for each of our ten home games during the playoffs. Certainly, with such support, it was clear that pro basketball had come to stay in Southern California.

Perhaps we were overconfident and looking past the early rounds to the final, but we got off to a horrible start in the playoffs, losing the first two games at home to San Francisco. This shook us up and just when everyone was writing us off, we won four straight to take them out. Three of those games were on the Warriors' court. We held them below 100 points in each of the last four games and beat them by 40 points in the last game. Thurmond dominated Wilt at the outset, but then Wilt asserted himself. I averaged more than 30 a game and felt good going into the second round.

Atlanta is a physical team and gave us a tough series in that second round, but we defeated them in five games. Each of these games was ruggedly contested. I was double-teamed most of the time and averaged only 20. Every time I turned around I was staring at a couple of guys who were bumping me. Still, the other Lakers did a whale of a job and we held the Hawks below 100 points three times. Wilt was enormous in the final, hauling down 29 rebounds and blocking shot after shot in the closing minutes.

Over in the East, Boston had blown Philly out in five, then after New York had blitzed Baltimore four straight, Boston stopped the Knicks in six. So, after the long season, here it was Boston and L.A. again, in the finals for the sixth time. Certainly there was a mental problem to overcome, since we had never topped them in the playoffs. However, this was an aging Boston team which figured to be tired. And we had beaten them four out of six during the season and the last time by almost 40 points. And having had the superior season record, for the first time we had the home court advantage. We had the first two at home and, if it went that far, four of the seven, including the last one, at home.

The opener probably was one of the greatest games in basketball history. Both teams moved the ball well, shot well and made few mistakes and the score was close during the full 48 minutes. I wish I could have been one of the Forum-record 17,554 fans in the stands watching this one. I had to play, of course, and played well, breaking my own NBA record for points by a guard in a playoff game by one with 53, the second best total of my career.

However, I shot much more than usual, 41 times. I got the openings and felt like I could hit with little Em Bryant guarding me, so I kept shooting, but I've shot better and I missed 20. Elg got 24 points. We won, 120-118, despite 37 by Havlicek, who is a great clutch player and seems to be tireless.

In the second game, I came back with 41, but Havlicek got 43. However Elg came up with his greatest game of the play-offs with 32 points, while Egan popped in 26 and we won, 118-112. Elg scored our last 12 points and you had to feel good for him. Another Forum-record crowd of 17,569 whooped it up.

Now we had them by two, but had to go to Boston. I fell in the last few minutes of that second game and banged my right hand. It swelled up pretty bad, but as it turned out it didn't bother me too much the rest of the way. They switched to bigger men on me like Havlicek and they started dropping off a second man on me whenever possible, but I found I could drive on Russell by going around him and using my long arms to throw up reverse layups so I did that a lot and when I was double-teamed I just fed off to the open man.

I guess it was Boston's turn and they beat us, 111-105, in the third game in Boston Garden. I got only 24, while Havlicek got 34 and Larry Siegfried came off the bench to bang in 28. They always have men coming in who can hit and spark a rally. After this game, we began to use Erickson at forward in-stead of the inexperienced Hewitt to defense Havlicek and that did slow him down some. It gave us a chance to win the fourth game, which would have been a big win.

The fourth game was a bad ball game. Both teams played poorly. The scoring was terrible. I got 40, but as a team we got only 88. Still, we had them by one point with 15 seconds to play and we had the ball. There is no way we should have lost. It was inexcusable. Baylor threw the ball in to Egan from out of bounds, but Bryant banged into him and took the ball away from him. Jones threw up a shot which missed and Wilt tipped the ball toward the sidelines to Baylor but the referee ruled Baylor had stepped out of bounds trying to save it and awarded it to Boston.

After the time-out, there were only seven seconds left. Bry-ant passed in to Havlicek, who passed to Sam Jones, a great clutch shooter, who figured as the best bet to take the last shot. Sam, who was retiring after the playoffs, broke behind a screen set up by Bailey Howell. Howell blocked me off on defense, but I reached for Jones anyway. And Jones bumped into Howell. Sam was off balance when he shot and he seemed to just throw the ball up. It went high, but short. It hit the front rim. But it bounced up in the air, came down, hit the back rim and fell through. The buzzer sounded and it was all over, 89-88.

The crowd went wild. We went off unable to believe what had happened to us. I've seen sad, quiet dressing rooms, but I want to tell you that was one of the worst. Sam said later his shot was lucky, but their shots that look lucky always seem to go in. The fact is, if they were lucky to win, we would have been lucky to win, too. Neither side played well. Someone asked me what I thought and all I could say was I guess if the good Lord wants you to win, you win. We played dumb and so we lost. Had we won and gone home with the lead three games to one, I think we'd have won the series for sure. But you never know.

Now we were all square at two each and it was a depressing plane ride home for us, while Boston, given new life, must have felt pretty good. I felt that a loss like that would prove what we had. We'd either give up or become a better team for it. And we did bounce back. At home before a near-record home turnout of 17,553, we took them apart, 117-104. Wilt was just great, giving us three and four shots at a time and cutting them off at one shot. We had 17 more shots. I started cold, but got hot, scoring 39, 28 of them in the second half when I hit 10 in a row at one point. Egan and Erickson chipped in real well and Boston seemed worn out. From then on, I couldn't help thinking had we won that fourth game it would have been all over.

In the third period of that fifth game, Em Bryant stuck a finger in one of Wilt's eyes during a battle for a rebound and it affected his vision from then on. Then, in the fourth period, with only three minutes left to play, with the game won, I lost a little control of the ball on a dribble under the pressure of a press put on by Bryant and made a lunge for the ball and pulled a hamstring muscle in my left leg. I tried to run back on defense, but it hurt. I asked out and went down to the dressing room where the doctor looked it over. At first I didn't think it was serious, but when I realized it was it was depressing. We had won a big game and now led, three games to two, but we did not have a happy dressing room.

We went back to Boston and I was determined to play, though I didn't know how well I could play. Actually, it didn't seem a real bad pull and I've had worse injuries, but if it hadn't been in the playoffs I'd have benefited by some rest. The doctor shot me with cortisone right after the fifth game and novocaine right before the sixth game. My leg felt sort of dead. I couldn't drive off it or get the height on my jumps. However, it got better as I played and loosened up. I scored 17 of my 26 points in the second half. By then, we were beat. If I could have played a normal game, we would have won. As it was, Boston won a sort of mediocre game, 99-90.

So it was back to L.A. for the final. In winning 10 of the last 12 championships, Boston had been forced to a seventh game in a playoff series nine times and had won all nine. The year before they had come from behind one game to three to beat Philly and Wilt in seven and had won the seventh in Philly. And we had lost the last game of a playoff series to Boston at home before. However, this was the first time we had a seventh game at home, and if my leg held up, I thought we'd win. I don't really know why. Maybe I just wanted to feel that way. But I thought we'd win.

I was very tense all the day of the final game and Jane tried very hard to stay out of my way and to keep the kids out of my way. I was as thick with emotion going into the game as I ever have been. They had given Sam Jones a great ovation when they introduced him for the last time in Boston, and now the L.A. fans gave him a great ovation when they introduced him for the last time in L.A. I was introduced last, which was unusual, and I got the greatest ovation of my life, a standing ovation. I guess it was because of my playing with the injury and all, but I want the people to know now I appreciate it. However, then, it bothered me. I moved away, like to hide. I just wanted to get on with the game.

The leg felt better. For awhile, we didn't play too bad, though we've played better. Under pressure, Boston was very poised. At first they shot well. In fact, guys like Sam Jones, who often shoots well, and Em Bryant, who is not considered a great shooter, couldn't seem to miss from outside. We kept falling 10 or 12 points behind, but kept fighting back. At the end of the first half we were only one point back, but Hawkins fouled Sam Jones right at the buzzer at midcourt and he picked up a couple of free throws to move the Celts three up.

Still, we didn't figure the Celtics could keep shooting as well as they had been, and since we'd been able to stay close up to then, we felt we could take them in the second half. And early in the second half, we caught them at 60-all. Then we had an unbelievable streak when we couldn't hit for five minutes. We missed 15 or 16 straight shots. It was partly my fault. I missed only one, but should have shot more. They kept pulling further and further ahead of us and had us by 15 after three periods and 21 by well into the last period.

We didn't give up. They finally cooled off and we began to come back. They'd shoot and miss and we'd come back and shoot and score. Little by little, their lead shrunk. Suddenly, we had the momentum. Wilt began to limp badly and was taken out, but we kept going. I felt like I couldn't miss. Everything I threw went in. Counts, subbing for Wilt, threw in a big one and we pulled to within one point at 103-102, and the crowd of 17,568, which was just waiting to explode in a victory celebration, was really throwing down the noise.

On the bench, apparently, Wilt asked back in, but the coach decided to stand pat because we were going well. I can't fault that. Counts threw in another basket which would have given us the lead, but it was taken away from us when he was given a close call for traveling. I missed a shot. And I lost the ball when I dribbled it off Bryant's knee. I stole a lot of balls and passed off for a lot of assists throughout the series, yet I'll remember the ball I lost long after I've forgotten the good plays.

They brought the ball back and missed a shot and the rebound came way out. Don Nelson picked up the garbage and threw it back toward the basket. It bounced off the rim five or ten feet in the air and came right straight down through the basket. When they need it, they always seem to get baskets like that. It put them three ahead again.

When we needed one, we couldn't get it. Counts tried to force in for a layup, but Russell blocked the shot. Erickson tried to pass in under the basket, but had it stolen. Siegfried was fouled and hit both free throws. Suddenly, Boston had five. We picked up a free throw, then a layup by Egan at the final buzzer, but it was all over, 108-106.

We had done everything we wanted to do right up to the last game. We won the division title and gained the playoff finals and outplayed Boston through much of the finals. But it came down to one game and we lost it. One game! We had a better team than Boston, I think. But we didn't prove it. We won more games than they did all season. But they won the last one. They ran off happily. We walked off miserably.

Russell came to me and held my hand and Havlicek and others came to me to say nice things and I'm grateful for such things now, as I will be the rest of my life, but just then it didn't help ease the pain much.

I sat in the dressing room and the writers told me I'd scored 42 points and had broken the record with 556 points in the playoffs, but it left me cold.

Sport Magazine had a Dodge car to give to the Most Valuable Player in the playoffs. All through the playoffs, honestly, I hadn't given it a thought. I figured it would go to a member of the winning team. If we won, that would be the big thing. If I got the car, great, but it would just be gravy. Now Al Silverman of *Sport* came to me to tell me I'd been named to get the car, and it left me cold.

Really, this was quite an honor, especially for a member of the losing side, and I know I'll always appreciate the individual recognition I received in this series, but Al will have to pardon me when I say I'd have given him the car if he or anyone else could have given me the championship.

Later, someone pointed out that because we'd finished higher during the regular season, we'd actually gotten a little more money out of the playoff pot than Boston. I earned the $8,000 or so that was my share, but the money was meaningless. You can't buy titles.

I guess it just wasn't meant for me to be a member of a championship team. Maybe there'll be another year, another chance. I don't think so right now. Maybe I'll think differently another time, but then I sat in that awful, still dressing room listening to the noise of the Boston players celebrating as it came through the walls and it was like I'd been hit by this all my life and now I'd been hit one time too many. Russell had 11 titles. I had none. The Celts had beaten the Lakers in the finals six times, in a seventh game four times. I've been disappointed before, but this was the worst because it was the last time. I admire Russell and Havlicek and Jones and all the great Celtics, who always have it when it counts, and I envy them. I didn't cry, but I wanted to.

I guess it just wasn't meant for me to be a member of a championship team. DARRYL NORENBERG

16
A Very Special Agony

My nose has been broken eight or nine times. My hands have been broken twice. I've broken fingers. I've pulled and torn muscles. I've twisted and sprained my fingers, my wrists, and my ankles. I've been bruised from head to toe and once I bruised my hip so badly I couldn't play. Usually, I play. We all play on nights we don't feel well.

Sometimes you can't play. I missed 25 games in 1963, 14 games in 1967, 31 games in 1968, 21 games in 1969 and others in other seasons—128 in nine seasons as a pro.

The NBA plays a long season of nearly nine months which begins with exhibitions in September and ends with playoffs in May. This is just plain too long. The NBA should figure out a way to cut a month off the season and reduce the number of games to give the players adequate rest from time to time. In the 1969 season, the Lakers played 100 regular-season and playoff games, plus 13 exhibitions. Only when the season is over do we get to mend our wounds.

I think pro basketball players are the best-conditioned athletes in sports. They retire younger and have shorter careers than football, hockey or baseball players. Sam Jones was the oldest player in the league when he retired at the age of 35 following the 1969 season, after just 12 years in pro ball. Bill Russell, a few months younger and a veteran of 13 seasons, was talking about playing several more years. Winning championships kept both men young. But older men were still active after longer careers in other sports. How many fat basketball players have you seen? Maybe trackmen like sprinters and milers are more sharply tuned to the limits of their physical ability, but there are some fat men among the shot-putters and discus-throwers. We run the fat off.

I don't like to remind people how many injuries I've had. It can sound as if I'm asking for a crying towel. I'd rather remind people that I've led the Lakers in minutes played. And I've missed only two playoff games in my entire career. But I can't write a book and not talk about my injuries.

I've had worse injuries than the torn hamstring muscle in the 1969 playoffs. Still, it limited me, and I worry that I might have done permanent injury to the muscle since I wasn't able to feel it quite properly after the injections of pain-killer.

A broken nose is a severe handicap, too, although people don't realize it, possibly because it doesn't prevent me from playing. It hurts worst the first day you've broken it and it's stuffed with cotton.

The first time I broke my nose—in college, in the Kentucky tournament—the doctor straightened it out and taped it right after the game. Back in Charleston, the doctor said it hadn't been set right and he'd have to do it over again. He just did it, without any anesthetic. I almost jumped off the table. It was the most painful thing I've ever endured. It was a cruel way for him to do it.

Usually they manipulate the nose, trying to pull it back into place. It's not easy to get it straight because my nose by now is pretty crooked. All I ask is that they make sure it's pointed in the right direction.

I've had a minor operation, but I'm saving the real nose job until after I quit playing. There's no point in being made beautiful now if I'm just going to run into Willis Reed again. He's broken my nose twice. Once more and he gets permanent possession of me.

I've played with a protective glove on my hand. I've played

with bandages and face masks and nose guards, but these things are heavy and cumbersome and affect my vision. They annoy me, so I don't use them. This is my livelihood and I have to go at it the way I can do my best.

It's not as if I was in any real danger. I'm not a race-driver or a bullfighter or someone who can get killed doing his thing. I don't have to stand in there against brush-back pitches like a baseball player, who can possibly get killed too. I can only get hurt. Or have my career cut short.

I get lots of advice from amateurs who are deeply interested in my welfare and the team's welfare. When I was injured in the 1969 playoffs, two well-meaning ladies called up to offer special solutions in which I could bathe and immediately be restored to perfect health. And an aging and bent man came to the door to offer some salve which he said had restored him to peak condition and could do the same for me. I let Jane handle such offers. I'm not very patient with people when I'm hurt. And I know I'm beyond the reach of home remedies.

I get excellent care. The Lakers' doctors, Dr. Robert Kerlan and Dr. Frank Jobe, and the team's trainers, Frank O'Neill and also Charley Saad, and all the others who have patched me up, have done their best for me. I guess I'm beyond medical science, too.

I hate it when people say I'm injury-prone. But it's time to make a confession. I now admit what I've denied, not only publicly, but to myself, for so long: I think I am injury-prone.

I do play aggressively, but I like my life and my limbs and I don't think I do things many other athletes don't do, yet they don't get hurt as often as I do. Maybe it's just been chance that I've had so many injuries, and I'm just unlucky.

Whatever it is, what can I do? Give up? Quit? Injured, I've thought about quitting many times. But as I recover, the mood passes. One of these days, it may not.

Some say little men get hurt more than big men, but I don't believe that. The fact is, there aren't many little men in pro basketball. There are players who are smaller than most in pro basketball, but these are still big men by ordinary standards, well-conditioned men, strong men, tough men.

I'm 6-3 and weigh almost 190 pounds. I look skinny and most people don't realize how big I am. If I was a professional boxer, I'd have to fight heavyweights. I'm even big enough to be an end or a back in pro football. I'm bigger than most hockey or baseball players.

It is true that I give away inches and pounds to most others on court. Because of this, I can't push them around. But this doesn't pull my muscles or break my nose. I do go at them hard, but I only know how to play the game one way. I can't change. If I could it wouldn't matter. I couldn't try to protect myself and play well. No one could. I just have to take my chances, like everybody else.

Basketball was not a well-conceived game. It was designed as a non-contact game of skill, in which it would be difficult to score. But it's not played that way, especially on the pro level. On the pro level, it is a high-scoring game of considerable body contact.

Big men play in cramped quarters on a small court. They lean and grab and push and pull. They run hard and move hard. In scrambles for loose balls or rebounds, the collisions are awful.

Actually, we beat each other up out there. Honestly, I have no objection to this. But I do think we have to recognize and accept that this is what the game is, not what we used to think it was. That's my main objection to pro basketball. The people in it keep pretending the rough stuff is unusual. They keep pretending the game is something it's not.

The referees are caught in the middle. They have rules to follow, but they must use their judgment. Lately they've been using the guide "no harm, no foul." So everything comes down to individual interpretation. It's a very fast game and the refs have to make their decisions in split seconds. It's the hardest game of all to officiate.

I haven't said much about referees, not because I think

they're so good, but because they do a good job under difficult circumstances. I don't think the refereeing in the NBA is as good as it should be. But I think the NBA itself is responsible for this.

What the NBA needs more than anything else is to raise the standards of officiating. We have too many part-time, inexperienced referees. We don't have enough capable men to work with.

The NBA has to adopt firmer rules as to what the game is, how it should be played, what is to be permitted, and what is not to be permitted. The league has to seek out the best men, offer them enough money to get them and keep them on a full-time year-round basis. The NBA is old enough and big enough and rich enough for this now.

If pro basketball has become a game of seven-footers and 100-pointers, so be it. That's the game, the real game, and let's face it. If it's a game that's easy to master, fine. Some will still handle it better than others. You'll still have winners and losers.

Some guys are still going to outsmart others. They're not all mental marvels in this game. Maybe it's not as scientific a game as football, but guys haven't made it because they couldn't think fast enough.

I remember one player the Lakers had, who was pretty good physically but had nothing upstairs. We all knew it. The coach knew it. We have some set plays. Not too many—20 or 25. It doesn't take a genius to remember them, but this fellow couldn't.

In a time out, the coach would call for the play. He'd take pains to lay it out for this guy, even though we all were supposed to know it inside out. "Have you got it now? Do you know it?" the coach would ask. The player would say, "Sure, coach, sure. Don't worry. I got it."

Then the buzzer would blow and the guy would walk out on the court and sneak up to me and say, "Jeez, Jerry, what the hell am I supposed to do?" He's gone now.

As far as the game goes, we shouldn't raise the baskets. We

shouldn't legislate against the tall man. This is their game. It's fine that there's a place for them. There's still plenty of room for the little men. Many men smaller than I am can play it well. It's not that the little men can't do a job. It's just that some people have thought they couldn't, and they have passed this feeling on to the writers and the fans. It's wrong.

My main criticism of the concept of pro basketball as it is played today is that not enough opportunity is given to small men. If I had my chance to put together my ideal team, it would consist of one big man and four small men. I don't mean a giant surrounded by midgets. I mean one tall, agile, gifted guy and four smaller, but quick and aggressive men.

If you have two men of identical ability to choose from and one is 6-7 and one is 6-2, you have to take the taller man because he will give you more possession of the ball. But players aren't of identical ability. Usually the smaller men are quicker, more aggressive, more mobile. They'll steal the ball more, move it better, and shoot from more places.

You have to have the big man in the center. He controls the boards and he controls the game. He lets the little men play aggressively and gamble. Boston has won with smaller men than other teams used. The big man, Russell, always lets the smaller men gamble and play aggressively.

There's been nothing wrong with Havlicek at 6-5 playing forward. There's been nothing wrong with Baylor at 6-5 playing forward. I'd rather have had them than almost any 6-8 or 6-10 forwards I can think of. There's been nothing wrong with Len Wilkens at 6-1, or Jim King at 6-2, or Dave Bing at 6-3, playing guard. How many 6-5 or 6-6 guards are better?

We've gone too much to height in pro basketball, but I do think we're beginning to get away from it now. The coaches are beginning to see what a quick, aggressive little man can do. More than anything else, I like aggressive players and aggressive teams. I also like happy teams. If you've got a quick, aggressive, happy team, you've got a winning team, and if the players are as good as their rivals, you've got a championship team. That's what the Celtics have been all these years, good, quick, aggressive and happy.

Most of my years with the Lakers, we were quick, aggressive and happy, but not quite good enough. We won pennants, but not championships. It's just one man's opinion, but in my opinion the Lakers have made a lot of mistakes since I've been with them. The players are supposed to let the bosses run the show and shut up, but we're dependent on the men around us for how we do. It's our livelihoods and I think we have a right to speak out once in a while about how we feel.

The Lakers have made some bad draft picks and some bad player deals over the years. They've traded away some players and let some players go, mostly in expansion drafts, who were important to us. This is not second-guessing. Most of us objected to the moves when they were made. And most did turn out badly. And aside from the abilities of the men involved, these moves took away men who fit in, and broke up our happy family.

In the All-Star game in the middle of the 1967-68 season, the Lakers had a lot of players in it but most of them were ex-Lakers. These included Dick Barnett of New York, Bob Boozer of Chicago, Walt Hazzard of Seattle and Rudy LaRusso and Jim King of San Francisco.

LeRoy Ellis helped Baltimore. Don Nelson of Boston was a big help to them, as he was to us before we let him go. John Block showed some potential when he got to play regularly in San Diego. Gale Goodrich never got to play regularly with us but in the 1968-69 season after he went to Phoenix and got to play regularly he became an outstanding performer despite his lack of size. Darrall Imhoff and Archie Clark certainly helped Philly that season, too.

When you're in the position of trying to make decisions and deals that will build your team up, you're bound to make mistakes. I realize that. And some of my sentiment is personal. I missed Stumpy. I missed Darrall.

But I have to say that I think every veteran we've had has

felt that in trading players or exposing players to the draft, we too often let experienced players go in favor of promising second-stringers, often gave away better players than we kept or got, and seriously disrupted the style and harmony of our club.

We were always winning pennants, but we were not just building up toward a championship, we always seemed to be rebuilding.

Boston and Los Angeles have dominated the NBA for many years now, but other teams are beginning to catch up. Boston always makes shrewd player moves and if they get some help in the backcourt and especially if Russell continues to play, the Celtics will continue to be tough. However, I think New York, especially, and Baltimore are already just as tough. I think the Knicks are the coming team in basketball. They are well-coached and have the smartest starting five to play in this league in many years. They make very few mistakes. And Baltimore is almost as promising and could get better.

This league has more good players and is stronger now than ever in its history. There are more good young players than ever before. New York has many of them, including Willis Reed, Walt Frazier and Bill Bradley. Reed is exceptional and may be the next MVP in the league. Frazier could be a super-player. In the past, defensive players didn't get the credit they should have gotten, but I've been glad to see Frazier get some. He's superb on defense, a great ballhandler and passer and he can score. He should shoot more. I was skeptical about Bradley at first, though not about his shooting ability, but he's convinced me he's solid now. He does a lot of things real well and he's gained the confidence that has freed him to do them consistently.

Baltimore has two of the finest young players in Wes Unseld and Earl Monroe. Unseld won the players' vote as MVP in the league in 1969, a rare honor for a rookie, and after the Bullets were taken out of the playoffs in a hurry, a lot of people said he really didn't deserve it, after all. But I still feel he did, and so do most of the players to whom I've talked. He's an unusually smart and unselfish player who gets the ball off the boards for his team, and gets it out to start fast-breaks incredibly well. He's a key man. Monroe is primarily a scorer, but he's also a good passer and he does everything in such a flashy way that if I had to pay my way into pro basketball games, he's one player I'd pay to see. He's really exciting to watch.

There are more good guards around today than there ever have been. I've mentioned Monroe and Frazier. Dave Bing is another, the kind of guy who can do a lot of things and has a chance to achieve real stardom. And Hal Greer is the sort who matures late and who never seems to get the credit he deserves, but is one of the best all-around and most consistent players in the game, and certainly one of the most underrated. There are others. And there are lot of good men up front, too —like Reed and Elvin Hayes, who have tremendous talent. If he applies himself, Hayes could be as good as any center before long. He can do anything—score, block shots, rebound. His main problem is that he may be on a team which will demand a lot of him in the next few years.

The same may be true of Alcindor as he comes in with Milwaukee. Hayes can overcome this problem. So can Alcindor. I think Alcindor will be the next dominating force in the NBA. He has a greater variety of shots and is a better shooter than any big center to come along so far. He has less strength than some, but more agility. I have said I think strength is important, but can be overrated in places, and even if Alcindor doesn't add weight and strength, his agility should more than make up for it. He really impresses me and I have no reservations about him whatsoever. He will be a super-star, for sure, and I wish him well, but I must say being a super-star does not always guarantee championships—and happiness—which are the same thing. Three so-called super-stars were not enough in 1969 to win a championship.

I plan to play a tenth year. One of the few specific goals I ever set for myself as an individual player was to score 20,000 points as a pro. It's only a figure, but it's one that always attracted me. It won't break my heart if I don't get it, but I'd like to get it. Counting regular-season games only, I was still nearly 3,200 points short after nine seasons. Counting playoffs, I was only 23 points short.

I've been around and I've gained experience which is very useful to me on court. I still work hard on my own game and there isn't a game in which I don't learn something I can use. Things happen so fast in this sport, you don't have time to think things out. I've reached the point where I find myself in the best position a lot of the time and I just have to react and it's usually all right. Positioning is as important as quickness. I'm still quick. I'm smoother handling the ball than I was earlier in my career. I'm a better player now than I ever was.

However, the strain of it is getting to me. The seasons seem longer than they ever did. And the injuries have really begun to bother me in recent years. Enduring these and working myself back into shape from each one depresses me. It's gotten so that people are afraid I'll trip over my crutches or get hurt just sitting on the bench, by falling off, and it's not funny. I've always been proud of the fact that I felt people could count on me on the court, but now I can see they feel they can't count on me to even make it to the court, and this irritates me. So I can't go on much longer.

I think I could coach. I've tried to learn and understand the game and I'm intrigued by the idea of fitting men into the best strategy and making the best substitutions and so forth. I hope I've earned some respect which would help me. It would be an interesting challenge and I'm not afraid of the pressure or the way coaches are pushed around. But I wouldn't do it just to do it. The situation would have to be right. With a college team. Or more likely a pro team. I'm too much of a perfectionist, too demanding, never satisfied with my own play or anyone else's, and I might not have the right temperament to handle men and handle the coaching job.

At times I've been skeptical about coaching. I've blown hot

and cold on it. I'll really miss van Breda Kolff coaching. I think he'll do well in Detroit. I would only hope that as a coach I could develop the same relationship with my players that he did. No coach could be a cinch to win with the Lakers or any other team, but the potential is certainly there in L.A.

In time I might be interested in becoming a general manager. The thing is, I'd like to stay around the game if I could. I could live without it somehow, but I know I'd really miss it. Jane and I have seen how it is with those who are out of it and how they miss being a part of it and how it hurts to be an outsider.

So I've kept playing, though I positively would not want to play one season, one game, even one minute after I felt I could no longer play my best or close to it, not for a big salary, not for anything. I know others have said it, but I mean it. I have too much pride for that. And it's that pride which turns me away from the game a little now. I've never won the big one.

There are many good reasons for playing this game, but the biggest and best of them is winning. If you can't do that, nothing else is enough. I've had many individual honors and the satisfaction of overcoming many injuries, but after coming close many times I still have never been on a championship team.

I'm not a satisfied person. I've achieved a great deal, I have a wonderful family and I lead a good life. But I'm the sort of person who never seems quite satisfied with anything, and after all the near-misses, I'm not even sure winning a team championship would satisfy me now. It might though. I'd take it. I want to tell you I'd cherish it. If I thought it was there for me somewhere for sure, I'd probably play ten more years looking for it.

Epilogue

There were times during the 1969 professional basketball playoffs when Wilt Chamberlain and Elgin Baylor did not seem old and worn, and played well. There were times when Johnny Egan and others carried their share of the load. But there were mostly times, especially under pressure in the finals against Boston, when Jerry West seemed to be bearing the burden of the Los Angeles Lakers' quest for victory all by himself.

By that concluding series, he had become the complete player—shooting with deadly accuracy, driving with uncanny skill, defending magnificently and rebounding, dribbling, and passing to perfection. He had become, in the eyes of many, the finest all-around performer who had ever played the game of basketball.

And in that series, he reaffirmed what he had long ago established, that he comes through in the clutch as perhaps no athlete ever has. His thigh muscles ripped, he endured agony through the final games, trying not to limp, trying not to make faces at the pain, trying not to give in to this thing that was damning his dreams. On one leg in the final game, he scored 42 points, took down 13 rebounds, passed off a dozen assists. But he could not do it alone. No team player in any sport ever could.

Jack Kent Cooke had hundreds of balloons encased in plastic containers and hung from the rafters to be opened at the moment of the championship triumph. He hired the University of Southern California marching band to sit silent throughout the contest just so they could strut the strains of

"Happy Days Are Here Again" at the instant of victory. He put cases of champagne on ice for toasts to the long-awaited success. A record crowd of more than 17,000 persons, many of them having paid scalper's fees to get in, waited to explode their pent-up emotions. Jerry was introduced last and got his greatest ovation, for the first time one greater than Elgin's. It bothered him. He lowered his eyes and scuffed his sneakers on the court and turned to the huddle. He wanted to get on with it, this title quest.

But in the end it was the Boston Celtics, as it has often been for more than a decade, who ran off the court as champions. And it was the Lakers, as it had been five times before, who hunched off with hung heads. Boston had five men, six men, seven men, eight men who could be cool in the heat of the final fire, while Los Angeles had only one, and maybe one or two others. Most feel the Lakers had more power. Some will replay plays in this game and tell you why it should have come out differently, but it did not, and you must conclude it doesn't matter. They own it—the Celtics and their fans.

The balloons still hung, going flat, in the rafters. The bandsmen packed up their instruments and shuffled quietly away. The champagne, unopened, grew warm. Jerry West, sore and sweaty and exhausted, sat on a bench in the silent Laker dressing room, his bum leg resting on a chair, and he said, "I can't believe it. I still can't believe it happened. Not this time now. Not again." His voice was thin and soft and ached. "I guess it just wasn't meant to be. I guess I just wasn't meant to play on a champion, to be part of a championship team." He turned to where the sounds of the Celtic celebration pressed through the walls and he said, "I can't stand to listen to that."

They came to him, the Celtics, to tell him what they felt of him and for him. Bill Russell could not speak, but he took Jerry's hand and squeezed it and held it for what seemed an eternity. And John Havlicek came up to him and said, "I love you." And later, Havlicek said, "I am only sorry that that man could not have played on a championship team." And K.C. Jones said, "He is a beautiful man and I only wish I could have apologized every time I fouled him."

Upstairs, in the press lounge where the wives waited for the players, many wept, including Jane West. She tried to control herself. Her pretty face was drawn and her lips quivered and her eyes kept brimming with tears and she said, "It's such a shame, such a darn, rotten shame. He wants it so much and deserves it so much and he can't have it. No one ever wanted it as much or deserved it more and he can't have it. I feel so sorry for him."

He came to her quietly and took her home.

And a few days later they flew to New York to pick up Jerry's car—colored, incredibly, in Celtic green. "It doesn't mean anything to him," Jane kept saying. "Nothing does except the championship which he can't have. No honors can make up for that." But there are some things which no one can ever take away from him, as the Celtics have taken championships. And in a corner of this man there is a pride indicative of the tributes paid him.

In *Sports Illustrated*, Frank Deford writes, "He is the most human star in sports." Fred Schaus, who coached him so many years, says, "He gives more of himself than any man I've ever known." Bill van Breda Kolff, who came from Princeton to coach the Lakers, notes, "I have high ideals of what a man and a player should be. Jerry West fits these ideals." And Jack Kent Cooke: "He is just about the perfect example of all that is good in an athlete and in a person."

Elgin Baylor marvels, "It doesn't seem possible that we could have shared the burdens and spotlight so long and never had a cross word, but with West it has been possible." Rod Hundley, who also played with him, a swinger who could never get Jerry to swing with him, smiles and says, "Jerry keeps saying he wishes he was more like me. What he doesn't know is I wish I was more like him."

Jerry West's mother says, "He's always wanted perfection. I think he's come closer to it than most. But I doubt that he's satisfied. He's still the boy he always was, who wants to be perfect and just can't understand why he can't be." And Jerry's wife adds, "I think he is as good as he is, as good as a man can be, as a husband, as a father, as a son, as a friend, as a performer, as a person, because he wants to be good so very much. I only hope basketball will miss him as much when he goes as he will miss it."

But he is not gone yet. He leaves for the arena, riding

through the evening light. When he gets there, the beautiful building is sparkling, but inside it is quiet for it is early yet and the fans are just beginning to arrive. He walks through the carpeted entrance and down an inside stairway and through a gloomy corridor to the dressing room, responding politely to those who speak to him as he passes.

In the dressing room, he greets the other players, kidding with them. He goes to his cubicle, takes off his civvies and slowly pulls on his gaudy uniform. He sits there for a moment, watching big Wilt, Elg, and the others. He rubs a sore and discolored thigh and turns to the trainer, who tapes it tight while Jerry winces.

He sits on the stool with his hands clasped between his bony knees, closes his eyes and bends over in thought. The tension has grown all day and now it is knotted through him, making him sick. How often has he gone through this? Nearly 1,000 times now. Yet he wants the next victory as much as he wanted the first one. And he dreads the next loss as much as he hated the first one.

It is not as bad now as it used to be, this very special agony, which is there for him to inflict on himself, and which he has suffered for so long, and which he will perhaps even miss when he passes from the game. But he is scarred inside and out by injuries and frustrations and disappointments and there is little hope in him now that the championship ever will be his. He is past 30 now, past his prime, better than he ever was on the court, but worn out now by all that goes with the playing of this game.

He pops some pills in his mouth to settle himself. He rubs his sore leg. He has been through it for so long and he is used to it by now, but it is always different, always a new challenge. The great moments, and there have been many, come and go. The bitter moments, and there have been many, come and go. But he goes on yet awhile.

The coach has been speaking, and he is done now, and he claps his hands. Jerry's boyish face is intense as he gets up and goes out with the others, onto the brightly lit hardwood court. The basketball thuds hollowly off the floor and then is sent spinning through the smoky air toward the hoop. The noise of the fans bangs down on the players.

Bill Libby

Appendix

JERRY WEST CAREER STATISTICS
(Through 1968–69 season)

VARSITY SCORING TOTALS

Team	Seasons	Games	FG	FT	Pts.	Average
East Bank H.S.	3	60	588	377	1,553	25.8
West Virginia U.	3	93	843	623	2,309	24.8
L.A. Lakers						
(Regular season)	9	613	5,933	4,969	16,830	27.4
NBA Playoffs	9	100	1,145	856	3,146	31.4
Pro Totals	9	713	7,078	5,825	19,976	28.0
CAREER TOTALS	15	866	8,509	6,825	23,838	27.5

OTHER TOTALS
(Not including high school)

	Games	Minutes	Avg.	Rebounds	Avg.	Assists	Avg.
West Virginia U.	93	3,138	33.7	1,240	13.3	261	2.8
L.A. Lakers							
(Regular season)	613	24,236	39.5	3,986	6.5	3,467	5.6
NBA Playoffs	100	4,230	42.3	651	6.5	567	5.7
Pro Totals	713	28,466	39.9	4,637	6.5	4,034	5.6
TOTALS	806	31,604	39.2	5,877	7.2	4,295	5.3

SHOOTING PERCENTAGES
(Not including high school)

	FGA	FG	Pct.	FTA	FT	Pct.
West Virginia U.	1,660	843	50.8	851	623	73.2
L.A. Lakers						
(Regular season)	12,670	5,933	46.7	6,133	4,969	81.0
NBA Playoffs	2,357	1,145	48.5	1,062	856	80.6
Pro Totals	15,027	7,078	47.1	7,195	5,825	80.9
TOTALS	16,687	7,921	47.4	8,046	6,448	80.1

235

VARSITY SEASONAL RECORDS

East Bank High School

Season	Class	Games	FG	FT	Pts.	Avg.
1953-54	Soph.	8	9	5	23	2.8
1954-55	Jr.	24	207	175	589	24.5
1955-56	Sr.	28	372	197	941	33.6

West Virginia University

Season	Class	Games	FGA–FG	Pct.	FTA–FT	Pct.	Pts.	Avg.
1957-58	Soph.	28	359–178	49.6	194–142	73.2	498	17.8
1958-59	Jr.	34	656–340	51.8	320–223	69.7	903	26.6
1959-60	Sr.	31	645–325	50.4	337–258	76.0	908	29.3

Los Angeles Lakers

Season	Year	Games	FGA–FG	Pct.	FTA–FT	Pct.	Pts.	Avg.
1960-61	1	79	1,264–529	41.8	497–331	66.6	1,389	17.6
Playoffs		12	202– 99	49.0	106– 77	72.6	275	22.9
1961-62	2	75	1,807–799	44.2	926–712	76.9	2,310	30.8
Playoffs		13	310–144	46.4	150–121	80.7	409	31.5
1962-63	3	56	1,213–559	46.1	477–371	77.8	1,489	26.6
Playoffs		13	286–144	50.3	100– 74	74.0	362	27.8
1963-64	4	72	1,529–740	48.4	702–584	83.2	2,064	28.7
Playoffs		5	115– 57	49.6	53– 42	79.2	156	31.2
1964-65	5	74	1,655–822	49.7	789–648	82.1	2,292	31.0
Playoffs		11	351–155	44.2	155–137	88.4	447	40.6
1965-66	6	79	1,731–818	47.3	977–840	86.0	2,476	31.4
Playoffs		14	357–185	51.8	124–109	87.9	479	34.2
1966-67	7	66	1,389–645	46.4	686–602	87.8	1,892	28.7
Playoffs		1	0	0	0	0	0	0
1967-68	8	51	926–476	51.4	482–391	81.1	1,343	26.3
Playoffs		15	313–165	52.7	169–132	78.1	462	30.8
1968-69	9	61	1,156–545	47.2	597–490	82.0	1,575	25.8
Playoffs		18	423–196	46.3	204–164	80.4	556	30.8

HIGH-POINT GAMES

East Bank High School

(35 points or more)

Junior Year	Opponent	FG	FT	Pts.
Feb. 4, 1955	At DuPont H.S.	12	14	38
Feb. 22, 1955	Stonewall Jackson H.S.	15	7	37
Dec. 21, 1954	E. Bank Alumni	15	6	36
Senior Year				
Dec. 21, 1955	Stonewall Jackson H.S.	18	9	45
Jan. 4, 1956	At Charleston Catholic H.S.	18	9	45
Mar. 23, 1956	Mullens H.S. at Charleston (T)	16	11	43
Dec. 13, 1955	Beckley H.S.	15	10	40
Dec. 10, 1955	At Oak Hill H.S.	16	7	39
Mar. 24, 1956	At Morgantown H.S. (T)	15	9	39
Feb. 7, 1956	At South Charleston H.S.	16	6	38
Feb. 10, 1956	Dunbar H.S.	15	6	36
Dec. 24, 1955	At Nitro H.S.	17	2	36
Dec. 4, 1955	DuPont H.S.	12	14	36
Jan. 6, 1956	Clendenin H.S.	15	5	35

(T)—State Championship Tournament.

WEST VIRGINIA UNIVERSITY
(35 Points or more)

	Opponent	FG	FT	Pts.
Soph Season				
Jan. 8, 1958	At Villanova	11	15	37
Junior Season				
Dec. 29, 1958	At Tennessee	17	10	44
Mar. 20, 1959	At Louisville (TT)	12	14	38
Feb. 27, 1959	Wm. & Mary at Richmond (CT)	13	12	36
Mar. 13, 1959	St. Joseph's at Charlotte (TT)	12	12	36
Dec. 20, 1958	At Kentucky	15	6	36
Feb. 7, 1959	Holy Cross	12	12	36
Feb. 21, 1959	G. Washington	16	3	35
Senior Season				
Jan. 30, 1960	Wm. & Mary at Norfolk	15	12	42
Feb. 17, 1960	At G. Washington	14	12	40
Jan. 13, 1960	Virginia	15	10	40
Feb. 1, 1960	At VMI	14	11	39
Dec. 18, 1959	St. Louis at Lexington	16	5	37
Mar. 12, 1960	St. Joseph's at Charlotte (TT)	12	13	37
Feb. 26, 1960	Wm. & Mary at Richmond (CT)	13	10	36
Feb. 8, 1960	NYU	12	11	35

(CT)—Southern Conference Tournament.
(TT)—NCAA Tournament.

Los Angeles Lakers
(45 or more points)

Date	Pro Yr.	Foe	FG	FT	Pts.
Jan. 17, 1962	(2)	New York	22	19	63
Jan. 29, 1965	(5)	Cincinnati**	21	11	53
Apr. 23, 1969	(9)	Boston (P)	21	11	53
Apr. 5, 1965	(5)	Baltimore (P)	16	20	52
Dec. 3, 1965	(6)	Cincinnati	16	19	51
Dec. 10, 1965	(6)	At Cincinnati	21	9	51
Jan. 24, 1962	(2)	Cincinnati	17	16	50
Nov. 3, 1962	(3)	At San Francisco	21	7	49
Apr. 3, 1965	(5)	Baltimore (P)	15	19	49
Feb. 17, 1968	(8)	Philadelphia**	19	11	49
Apr. 8, 1965	(5)	At Baltimore (P)	20	8	48
Dec. 17, 1961	(2)	Detroit at Minneapolis	18	11	47
Dec. 25, 1963	(4)	At New York	19	9	47
Jan. 26, 1965	(5)	At New York	18	11	47
Feb. 21, 1965	(5)	Boston	18	11	47
Feb. 5, 1962	(2)	Cincinnati at Morgantown	16	14	46
Dec. 1, 1962	(3)	At St. Louis	20	6	46
Nov. 17, 1965	(6)	Boston	15	16	46
Dec. 7, 1965	(6)	New York	14	18	46
Feb. 3, 1962	(2)	At St. Louis	14	17	45
Apr. 19, 1965	(5)	At Boston (P)	17	11	45
Apr. 22, 1966	(6)	Boston (P)	19	7	45
Jan. 25, 1967	(7)	Baltimore	16	13	45

(P)—Post-season playoffs.
**—Two overtimes.

RECORDS SET

*High School—Set all East Bank H.S. field goal, free throw, and total points records. First high school player in history of West Virginia to surpass 900 points in a single season. Set state records with 902 points and 32.2 scoring average in 1956.

*College—Set twelve West Virginia U. records with career totals of 2309 points, 843 field goals, 623 free throws, 1240 rebounds, 93 games, and a scoring average of 24.8 points, and seasonal totals of 908 points, 340 field goals, 258 free throws, 510 rebounds, a shooting percentage of 51.8, and a scoring average of 29.3. Fifth in nation in scoring in 1958.

*Pro—Regular-season: Holds NBA regular-season scoring record for guards in one game with 63 points vs. New York, Jan. 17, 1962. Led Lakers in scoring and free throws five times and minutes played three times. Holds NBA record for most free throws in one season with 840 in 1965-66.

Playoffs: Holds all-time NBA playoff record for highest scoring average at 31.4 points per playoff game over nine seasons. Ranks first in free throws made with 856; is second in total points and shooting percentage; third in field goals and assists, and fifth in total minutes played. Also holds single-season playoff record with 556 points in 1969 and best single-series average with 40.6 points per game in 1965. Has single-season playoff records with 31 consecutive free throws in 1965 and a total of 164 free throws in 1969. Holds NBA record for guards for most field goals in one game with 21 and most points in one game with 53, both in 1969, surpassing his own previous records of 20 field goals and 52 points in one game in 1965.

SPECIAL HONORS

*High School—All-West Virginia, 1956.

*College—All-American first team on nine selections in 1959. Member of championship U.S. Pan-American Games team in Chicago, 1958, and Olympic Games team in Rome, 1960.

*Pro—All-NBA first team six straight seasons, 1962-67.

TEAM RECORDS

Team	Season	Class	Won-Lost	Finish
East Bank H.S.	1953-54	Soph.	16-4	Eliminated fourth state playoff game.
	1954-55	Jr.	11-13	Eliminated third state playoff game.
	1955-56	Sr.	23-5	Won state championship.
HIGH SCHOOL TOTALS			50-22	One state title.
	Season	Class		
West Va. U.	1956-57	Fr.	17-0	No post-season play.
	1957-58	Soph.	26-2	Won Southern Conf. Ranked No. 1 nationally. Eliminated first NCAA tourney game.
	1958-59	Jr.	29-5	Won Southern Conf. Eliminated fifth and last NCAA tourney game.
	1959-60	Sr.	26-5	Won Southern Conf. Eliminated third NCAA tourney game.
COLLEGE TOTALS		Varsity—81-12		Won three conference titles.
		All—98-12		One NCAA title runner-up.
	Season	Year		
L.A. Lakers	1960-61	1	36-43	Second Western Division
	Playoffs		6-6	Eliminated second round, by St. Louis.
	1961-62	2	54-26	Won Western Division.
	Playoffs		7-6	Lost, 4-3, in finals, to Boston.
	1962-63	3	53-27	Won Western Division.
	Playoffs		6-7	Lost, 4-2, in finals to Boston.
	1963-64	4	42-38	Third Western Division.
	Playoffs		2-3	Lost first round to St. Louis.
	1964-65	5	49-31	Won Western Division
	Playoffs		5-6	Lost, 4-1, in finals, to Boston.
	1965-66	6	45-35	Won Western Division.
	Playoffs		7-7	Lost, 4-3, in finals to Boston.
	1966-67	7	36-45	Third Western Division.
	Playoffs		0-3	Eliminated first round by San Francisco.
	1967-68	8	52-30	Second Western Division.
	Playoffs		10-8	Lost, 4-2, in finals, to Boston.
	1968-69	9	55-27	Won Western Division
	Playoffs		11-7	Lost 4-3, in finals, to Boston.
PRO TOTALS	Regular Season		422-302	Five Western Division titles.
	Playoffs		54-53	Twice second. Twice third.
	All		476-355	Five times title runner-up.

WEST'S TEAMS' TOTALS (all classes)   624-389